Thanks for Everything

HORNS UP!!

HORNS UP!!

COLLEGE BANDS OF THE ARKANSAS HEARTLAND

T. T. Tyler Thompson

Fanfare by W. Francis McBeth

PHOENIX INTERNATIONAL, INC.
FAYETTEVILLE

ISBN-13: 978-0-9768007-2-9

Cover concept by T. T. Tyler Thompson
Cover photos by Dixie Knight Studio
Graphics by LaserImages
Author's photo by Artisan Life Photography

Library of Congress Cataloging-in-Publication Data

Thompson, T. T. Tyler.
  Horns up!! : college bands of the Arkansas heartland / T. T. Tyler Thompson ; Fanfare by W. Francis McBeth.
      p. cm.
   ISBN-13: 978-0-9768007-2-9 (alk. paper)
   1. Bands (Music)—Arkansas—History. 2. Music in universities and colleges—Arkansas—History. I. Title.
   ML1311.7.A7T56 2006
   784.8'309767—dc22
                                                                        2006026017

This book is dedicated to all the men and women who, over the years, have brought the bands in this book to life, including my sister, Lee Thompson Berson, who served as a majorette in one of these bands (the answer as to which one is within these pages).

Seventy-six trombones led the big parade
With a hundred and ten cornets close at hand;
They were followed by rows and rows of the finest virtuosos,
The cream of ev'ry famous band . . .

from *The Music Man,* by Meredith Willson

Contents

Fanfare

This scholarly work is the definitive book on the history of bands in the Arkansas schools of higher learning. No research like this has ever been compiled before. It has taken the history of bands and universities from their beginnings to the present day. It has given equal attention to the growth of each college and university.

I entered the music scene in Arkansas in August 1957, and I have witnessed its progress since then. When I arrived, the Henderson State Band was led by Orville Kelley, the University of Central Arkansas Band by Homer Brown, the University of Arkansas at Pine Bluff Band by Harold Strong, the Arkansas State University Band by Don Minx, the Arkansas Tech Band by Gene Witherspoon, the Southern Arkansas Band by Richard Oliver, the University of Arkansas at Monticello Band by Quincy Hargis, the Harding University Band by Eddie Baggett, and the Ouachita Band by myself.

I had a close relationship with all these men, especially Gene Witherspoon. In 1957 Gene Witherspoon's Arkansas Tech Band was much more advanced than any of the others. In 1967 the Tech Band was invited to perform at the College Band Directors National Association Convention in Ann Arbor, Michigan. When the Tech Band had its first rehearsal in Ann Arbor, students in the Illinois and Michigan Bands, which were to play also, came to the rehearsal to laugh at this unknown band from Arkansas. The Tech Band was so good that the visiting students were shocked and Gene Witherspoon and the Tech Band acquired a national reputation overnight.

The Arkansas collegiate bands have had a few ups and downs over the past fifty years as a result of variations in funding, but the last fifteen years they have all been of excellent quality.

I wish to congratulate Dr. Thompson for his diligence in supplying us with this detailed treatise. It will remain as the definitive work on the college bands of the Arkansas heartland.

—W. Francis McBeth

Preface

Welcome to my second book about college bands in the state of Arkansas. And I digress here before I have barely started these pages, but have you ever wondered why the expression "college band" is used rather than "university band?" So many more of the latter are in the public eye across the country and so many more of them are connected to powerhouse athletic schools that I wonder why "university band" is not more the norm when referring to those musical groups of our schools of higher learning. But then again, I rarely hear radio and television sports announcers refer to the Saturday afternoon gridiron contests as being anything other than "college football" and the hoop fests in the winter and during March Madness as being anything other than NCAA college basketball—even when the great majority of schools participating in those sweat fests contain the word "university" in their names. I guess if I could explain the athletic reason above, I imagine I could simply extrapolate that over to the band question I posed first. But since I can't, I'll just restate my initial sentence: welcome to my second book about college bands in the state of Arkansas (even though the nine school bands discussed herein find residence on campuses that have been accredited with university status). I don't doubt that once this book hits distribution that I will receive a number of explanations to my above posed question, but probably none that will be any more successful in placating me than some of the "reasons" I have heard from friends when raising the subject with them.

That being said, I am very happy that this book is seeing the light of day. As I said above, it is my second one regarding the subject of college bands within the borders of my home state of Arkansas. My first book was about the Razorback Band at the University of Arkansas in Fayetteville entitled *The University of Arkansas Razorback Band: A History, 1874–2004*. I will admit to being positively prejudiced about that band since I was a member of said group from 1967 to 1971, serving as one of its drum majors for the last two seasons. I spent over five years researching the book's contents and can say that the experience was most eye opening as to the role the band has played and is playing in the life of that university campus. As was stated in the 1988 Razorback yearbook, the band members are "the background music makers of your educational career."

I cannot tell you how excited I was when I finally saw my Razorback Band book in print. The reality of holding it in my hands for the first time almost overwhelmed me (which I understand is not uncommon for any author who sees his or her first book in the flesh). At that moment, I was reminded of the time when I was a student on the campus of the U of A in Fayetteville studying at a table in Vol Walker Library. I noticed a professor a couple of tables over from me pouring over what looked to be a mound of old papers. Turns out that the professor was Robert Leflar of the Law School, and he was most diligently going about digging into his work. I was so amazed to see one of the pillars of the university plugging at his whatever-it-was-he-was-working-on with such industriousness, that all I could do was just stare at him. Soon, Dr. Leflar looked up from his papers and asked me, "Son, may I help you?" Being caught off guard, I said, "No. I was just wondering what it could be that has gotten your attention so." He sat back and replied, "Well, for your information, I'm working on a book about the first one hundred years of the University of Arkansas." For you, the reader, that would be the years encompassing 1871–1971, which indeed was covered in his book published in 1972 entitled *The First 100 Years: Centennial History of the University of Arkansas.* I said that I thought that that must be a fascinating bit of study, and he responded with a simple, "You have no idea." Before I returned to my own bookwork at hand, I commented that I'd sure like to be able to write a book some day. He took off his glasses, cleaned them gently with his handkerchief, and said, "Young man, first find something you are greatly interested in and find out everything you can about it. Then find a unique way to tell your story."

That day years later when I was holding my newly published book, I hoped that I had done just that, but I would have given almost anything to have been able to show it to Dr. Leflar and gotten his take on it. I will have to leave it to those today who have read it and accept their judgment as to its merits, but I feel satisfied that I gave it the old "college" or "university" try.

While attending a few book signings for the Razorback Band book, I heard gratifying comments from a number of people, but occasionally I entertained a comment like, "That's a nice book, but you know, we had a great band at Henderson," or "UCA," or "Arkansas Tech," or "..." Well, you get the picture. So I did some preliminary research on the other collegiate band programs within the borders of Arkansas to see how much information was there and if it could be assembled into a publication.

I discovered a number of music programs on the various college and university campuses in Arkansas. But what I needed to do was try and focus on a set of parameters within which I could solidly base a book. Sifting through the mounds of data that I had accumulated, I found that there are, as of this writing, nine college campuses in Arkansas other than the University of Arkansas at Fayetteville that have a band program in their curricula that offer both marching and concert band credits to their students. And that became the basis for this book.

I have organized those nine schools into three groupings.

The first group includes colleges that had their start as elementary and secondary teacher preparatory schools known at the time as "normal" schools. These are

Henderson State University, earlier known as Henderson State Teacher's College;
the University of Central Arkansas, previously known as Arkansas State Teacher's College; and
the University of Arkansas at Pine Bluff, known in earlier years as Branch Normal School, and later as Arkansas Agricultural, Mechanical and Normal College.

The second group includes colleges that had their start as district agricultural schools (in fact, they all began in 1909 with the passage of Act 100 by the Arkansas General Assembly and signed into law by Governor George W. Doneghey). These four schools are

Arkansas State University, known originally as the First District Agricultural School, and later as Arkansas State College;
Arkansas Tech University, known originally as the Second District Agricultural School, and later as Arkansas Polytechnic College;
Southern Arkansas University, known originally as the Third District Agricultural School, and later as Southern State College; and
the University of Arkansas at Monticello, known originally as the Fourth District Agricultural School, and later as Arkansas A&M.

The last grouping includes two private colleges that have marching and concert band programs on their campuses; they are

Ouachita Baptist University, a private college supported by and partially funded by the Arkansas Baptist Convention; and
Harding University, a private college supported by and partially funded by the Church of Christ denomination.

As I said, all of the above nine schools field a marching band and present a concert band on their campuses. In addition to marching and concert bands, each of the nine provides a pep band to play at intercollegiate basketball games and a jazz band program offering an additional nuance to the college band atmosphere.

That having been said, one might remark that there are or have been bands on some Arkansas college campuses that I haven't mentioned and you would be right. I'm just covering the ones that fulfill my criteria of having both a marching and concert band in their program.

For example, Hendrix College in recent years has had a Chamber Orchestra and Wind Ensemble, but no marching band. The campus had a marching band when it had a football team; but when the football team went defunct in the early 1960s, the marching band soon ceased to exist for lack of purpose. Photos above record the Hendrix Band during the 1913–14 school year at right and marching through the streets of Conway in the fall of 1950.

Philander Smith College in Little Rock began as a seminary in 1877 and had a music program available from its earliest days. Though it primarily involved a vocal and piano program in the beginning, there was a band on the campus as evidenced in the upper left photo dated sometime between 1900 and 1910. The upper right picture depicts the college's orchestra from the 1946–47 school year under the direction of L. W. Robbins. Though the band and orchestra programs faded in the second half of the twentieth century, in recent years a drum line has emerged on the campus to play at basketball games and to represent the Philander Smith College in various parades.

Also, in the early days of Little Rock Junior College (now the University of Arkansas at Little Rock), there was a band that cheered on the football team as shown in the above left photo from the school year 1932–33. But most often the group was a student-led pep band until the football team disbanded in the 1950s. A concert band program was offered on the Little Rock University campus (the school attained four-year university status in 1957) beginning in 1964 under the direction of Donald Kramer, shown above right, though the program was discontinued in the 1970s. Today the nineteen-member Trojan Pep Band directed by Chuck Law plays at on-campus intercollegiate basketball games. Also offered by the school's Music Department are opportunities to play in the Jazz Trio, Percussion Ensemble, and Community Orchestra.

Today, there is a very vibrant band program at the University of Arkansas at Fort Smith (once known as Westark Community College) under the direction of Charles Booker, encompassing a full concert band and a jazz band (*both shown above*) and a pep band for basketball. But there is no marching band due to the lack of a football team.

Lyon College in Batesville also at one time, when the school was known as Arkansas College, had an orchestra and a concert band on its campus, as shown in the above photos from the 1924–25 (*above left*) and 1947–48 (*above right*) school years. Today, no such program exists.

The above photo is evidence that there was also a band on the Arkansas Baptist College campus in Little Rock in 1917, but those days are long past. Among other schools in the state, John Brown University in Siloam Springs currently offers private lessons on some selected instruments to students as does the University of the Ozarks, but no formal band program is available on either of the latter two campuses.

Before I get into the specifics of the histories of each of the nine bands covered in the following chapters, the reader needs to be aware of the scarcity of bands on any level in the state of Arkansas during the late 1800s and early 1900s. The expense of the individual instruments was prohibitive for many people for personal use, and the school systems did not have surplus funds with which to back such a program in their curricula. As such, a band was an unusual occurrence at the time in the state, and when one did come into existence, it was a major event for a community.

If one remembers the story line of Meredith Willson's stage and movie musical, *The Music Man*, one may recall that when a music salesman came to town to start up a boys' band in River City, Iowa, the whole town was affected by the event. Well, the beginnings of boys' bands in Arkansas paralleled that story line to a point, except that the men and women trying to get the bands established in the state's communities weren't the shady characters as were posed in the musical. Those band pioneers knew about music, cared about their charges, and lived in the communities where they worked. An example was Fred D. Martin, who grew up in a large family in Arkadelphia as a member of the Martin Family Band, which his father had organized. As Fred approached manhood, he organized a fifteen-piece community band in Arkadelphia in 1922, which grew in two years to boast a membership of thirty-five. And in 1925 with a roster of one hundred and ten musicians, he took the band to Memphis to play for the national convention of the Rotarians. Though the band instruments were somewhat pricey, the boys and their families were able to participate in the program with the "easy payment plan."

Nearby Arkansas towns soon caught the band fever that Martin had begun, and members from those communities sought his expertise in starting similar bands in their hometowns. According to an article in the May 8, 1930, issue of the *Magnolia Banner-News*, Martin and his wife had organized twenty-eight bands in towns in Arkansas, Louisiana, Texas, and Missouri by that date. Obviously, with the Martin Bands growing in such popularity, Fred Martin could not direct them all, so he hired on a number of similarly talented men to share in the conducting duties, including L. E. Crumpler in Camden, Magnolia, and Waldo; L. B. Tapp, working out of Fayetteville in neighboring towns; C. R. Callendar, based in Texarkana, Texas; and Al Daniels, located in Arkadelphia. The legendary John Raymond Brandon, a founder and longtime executive director of the Arkansas School Band and Orchestra Association, also got his start in the band business as a Martin Band director.

Although not a part of the Martin Band structure himself, another Arkansas legend, R. B. "Scrubby" Watson, took over as director of the Pine Bluff High School Band in the 1930s from a Martin man who had started the group. Martin also had some influence in getting the bands started on the campuses of Ouachita College in Arkadelphia and the Magnolia A&M College (now Southern Arkansas University). Though not part of the Martin Bands business structure, Lee Wallick started a number of local community and school bands in a similar manner in the southeastern part of the state in addition to directing the college band on the Arkansas A&M campus. With time, bands in Arkansas came to be less of a novelty across the state and more as a fixture of pride for its communities.

Now, as to how those nine college bands covered in this book came into existence, I will try to do this chronologically. (I refer the reader to my previous book for the origins of the University of Arkansas Razorback Band in Fayetteville. This is a cheap plug, but a genuine reference.)

The University of Arkansas at Pine Bluff (also known affectionately by its older alumni as Arkansas AM&N) was originally established as a way to get around the requirement in the federal Morrill Act of 1862 that allowed that Land Grant schools could not discriminate as to student applicants with regard to race. When the university in Fayetteville got its start under the name of the Arkansas Industrial University in 1871 to finally open its doors after a couple of time extensions from the U.S. Congress, there was little interest by the white gentry of Arkansas to have both white and black students in the same classes. As a result, rather than encourage black students to attend the Fayetteville campus (though evidence shows that a few did apply and did enroll), the University Board of Trustees established a branch of the school in Pine Bluff which was the cultural and population center for the large number of black citizens in southeast Arkansas. The thought behind the trustees' intent was to offer education for black college students to eventually teach in black Arkansas primary and secondary schools. As far as a band at Branch Normal School, which was what the school was called at the time of its inception in 1873 and the opening of its doors to students in 1875, the founding superintendent, J. C. Corbin, was an avid musician and later formed an informal ensemble with some of his students. But the first official band was not organized on campus until 1902 by Corbin's successor, Isaac Fisher, consisting of 12 to 15 students. The band fluctuated between 25 and 50 musicians until the early 1950s. There was no military connection to the band during the early years of the school since the federal government did not actively recruit minorities into service at the time. Three directors who will always be linked with quality performances and establishing the roots of excellence manifested in the school's present music program are Alma Brown, Harold Strong and Odie Burris. Today the Golden Lion Band takes to the field with upwards of 270 students with John Graham as Director of Bands and is known as the "Marching Musical Machine of the Mid-South" or "M4."

There were only a few very small religious based colleges in Arkansas in the mid-1800s, among them six small associational Baptist schools scattered over the state with only two of them still open by 1886. At that year's annual meeting, the Arkansas Baptist Convention, after years of discussion, finally voted to establish a Baptist state college in Arkadelphia in the large single wood-framed structure near Arkadelphia Baptist High School that had been left empty when the Arkansas School for the Blind moved from the town to Little Rock. It was named simply Ouachita College after the river that runs through the area. As for a college band at Ouachita, its existence paralleled that which occurred on many American campuses at the time. In 1896 a Military Department was established on the campus with leadership from former Confederate officers, and uniformed male students began drilling regularly. Soon thereafter a band was organized to accompany these drills and eventual parades. And as the years progressed and organized sports joined the curriculum, the band also joined in supporting the teams with pep and spirit. Today the school's band is independent of its previous military ties and boasts greater than one hundred student members in the program under the direction of Robert Hesse and Dr. Craig Hamilton. But also important to remember in the band's legacy are the predecessors of the aforementioned gentlemen, Dr. W. Francis McBeth and Marvin Lawson. The current OBU Band refers to itself as "The Most Exciting Band in Tiger Land."

The physical grounds of the school known today as Henderson State University actually started out as Arkadelphia Methodist College in 1890, which proceeded along with measurable academic success until the state's Methodist Conference board merged it with Hendrix College on the Conway campus in 1929. Prior to that merger the school was known successively as Henderson College and Henderson-Brown College named after two board member benefactors who at various intervals contributed significant sums of money to the school's coffers. After the merger, the city of Arkadelphia approached the state legislature to open a new school in the college's remaining empty buildings, which was agreed to in time for the fall of 1929. Actually, with the great majority of the student body and faculty carrying over from the previous year, the school simply went from private school to public school status. The "merger" occurred mainly on paper and in the minds of the Methodist hierarchy. The "new school" was known as Henderson State Teachers College.

Instrumental music at the Methodist Henderson College began with an orchestra around 1903 and a regular band appeared in the early 1900s as an adjunct to the newly established Military Department. When the school reemerged in 1929 as Henderson State Teachers College, the band's director was T. J. Ashford, who was legally blind from birth, taught himself to play almost every instrument in the group, and memorized almost every piece of music he conducted after only a single hearing. Another man of distinction who held the position of Director of Bands at Henderson was the incomparable Wendell Evanson, having spent thirty years atop the school's podium. As with the other bands presented here, the Henderson State University Reddie Band is no longer associated with the school's military department and includes 150 musicians in the marching unit and 60 performers in the concert program. Its Director of Bands, David Rollins, resigned that position as of the end of spring semester 2006 having been at the school since 1988, allowing for a new person to take over the job. Henderson touts its band as being "The Showband of Arkansas."

The University of Central Arkansas started out as Arkansas State Normal School in Conway having been chartered in 1907 by the Arkansas General Assembly. It has been in the same basic location since its inception only having grown phenomenally over the years in acreage and population of student body and faculty. Unlike some Arkansas schools, women were members of the campus band from day one. Two "Homers" were instrumental in the band's success at different times in the group's life. Prof. Homer Hess was director of the group in the 1920s and 1930s, whereas Homer Brown was the school's beloved band director from 1958 to 1979. In fact, alumni band members who served under Brown today call themselves "Homer's Heros." Another director who distinguished himself on the UCA campus was Russell Langston, leading the band in the 1980s and early 1990s. The Bear Band is today challenged to support its school's athletic program, having moved from Division IIA to IAA in the fall of 2006. Presently, the band program under the leadership of Dr. Ricky Brooks serves upwards of 220 students each school year and is widely known as "The Sound of Central Arkansas."

As stated earlier four Arkansas colleges got their start in 1909 with the passage of Arkansas Act 100 as a result of the strong lobby of the Farmers' Union. At the time, high schools in the state were of such poor quality that the four schools were actually only envisioned to be high-quality high schools instructing students in agriculture, horticulture, and the art of textile making—in other words, outside farming and ranching for the males and inside homemaking and domestic skills for the females. Also during this time the explosion of the industrial revolution took place, and mechanical machinery created inroads to making farming more efficient. As years passed, the schools' emphasis adopted the mechanical aspect of education and their names changed to Agricultural and Mechanical Schools, hence A&M Schools, with all the students on the campuses initially known as Aggies (later as each school acquired its own identity, they also adopted individual mascots: respectively, they became and remain to this day the Indians, the Wonder Boys, the Muleriders, and the Boll Weevils). These glorified high schools eventually all achieved junior college status with the passage of Act 45 in the 1925 Arkansas General

Assembly with North Central Accreditation following shortly thereafter. And their names changed as their curricula expanded, the years of study increased from two to four years, and their sister preparatory schools closed, which had been associated with each school of higher learning, feeding graduated high school students to their programs.

So, the four schools started out as essentially advanced high schools emphasizing agriculture and home economics, morphing into junior colleges, then becoming full four-year colleges, and eventually state universities.

The first evidence of an instrumental group on the First District Agricultural School campus in Jonesboro is a photo of the 1923 school orchestra with a Miss Deal listed as its director. And in the fall of 1929 a band appeared on the campus playing at an on-campus football game with Guy French identified as its director. The campus ROTC program entered the picture in 1936 when the campus band started supporting field maneuvers. With the ROTC program on hiatus during World War II, the band program was also put on hold. But in 1946, the school's band revived, and today the all-civilian band numbers about 160 in its on-field marching performances. Few would deny that the ASU Band first established itself in the annals of excellence under the baton of Donald R. Minx from the 1950s to the 1970s. Today the growing band, under the recent guidance of Ed Alexander and Kenneth Carroll, is known as "The Pride of Arkansas State."

As for Arkansas Tech, the Russellville school had a band on campus early in the Second District Agricultural School's existence. In fact, the first student to enroll at the school was later drafted in 1913 to become its first band director, Marvin Williamson. Williamson continued as band director until 1950 and remained on the Tech faculty until 1956. In the mid-1930s the Tech Band also became tangent with the Military Department, but performs as an independent group today. Williamson's successor became a legend in the history of college bands in Arkansas. He was the one and only Gene Witherspoon, affectionately known as "Chief." Tech's current Director of Bands, Hal Cooper, has been in that position since 1979 and proudly oversees a program that includes 190 students in the marching program and 135 involved with the concert calendar. Tech proudly claims its band to be the "Band of Distinction."

The Third District Agricultural School, now Southern Arkansas University in Magnolia, was the last of the four agricultural schools to open. Where the other three opened in the fall of 1910, the Magnolia school didn't open until January 1911. The first instrumental group documented on the campus was the school's Cornet Quartet in 1913, with four distinguished-looking students posing with their personally owned instruments. Because all of the budding colleges had budgetary problems to some degree, it was much cheaper to offer choral classes or music appreciation courses in the Music Department than to offer instrumental challenges. Most students in the beginning years of the schools simply had to purchase their own instruments if they wanted to play in an orchestra or band program on campus. The first organized instrumental organization on the Mulerider campus appears to have occurred during the 1923–24 school year, as reflected in a photo from that year's yearbook. Apparently this school had a National Guard Company similar to its sister agricultural schools, as the band began servicing military drills and parades as early as 1933. Though the band also disbanded for a couple of years during World War II, it returned strongly in the late 1940s and remains a vibrant student organization today with about 125 students in its program, an increase of over 30 percent since the year 2000. Across the acres of the Magnolia campus, no band director's presence made a more lasting impression than three of its conducting icons: L. E. Crumpler, Richard Oliver, and Eddie Epperson, with Oliver having served the longest tenure. The present SAU Band, directed by J. P. Wilson, now takes to the field as "The Marching Mulerider Band."

The University of Arkansas at Monticello is the descendant of the Fourth District Agricultural School and today proudly boasts that its heritage indeed is one of agricultural excellence. Obviously, when those four schools were established, an emphasis on the arts did not have the highest priority for the administration and its trustees. But to the Monticello school's credit, there was a "directress of Music, Piano, and Voice," a teacher of piano and harmony, and a director of band and orchestra listed in the 1910 catalog. Professor Otto Mahling, the school's instrumental director, was a graduate of both the Conservatory of Berlin and the Conservatory of Vienna. One of Mahling's successors was Lee Wallick, a famous southeast Arkansas band director who not only was director of the Arkansas A&M Band for some time, but he also commuted to outlying towns in the area to create and direct high school and community bands in the afternoons and evenings. Oh yes, and he was also blind, a result of a board falling on his head during a building fire when he was a young man. Band music also disappeared on the A&M campus for a time during World War II, but it returned shortly after the war ended and has been there ever since, even though student participation has varied somewhat in the interim. Under the current direction of musical phenom Gary Meggs, over 140 Aggie Band members took to the field in the fall of 2005 under a banner that read, "The Spirit of Southeast Arkansas."

The ninth and final subject of this book about college bands in Arkansas is the band at Harding University in Searcy. Supported by the Church of Christ denomination, Harding actually got its start in Morrilton as Arkansas Christian College in 1922, which ended up having few students but good building facilities. At the same time in Harper, Kansas, the sister Church of Christ school, Harper College, had an adequate enrollment and strong faculty, but encountered problems with space and finances. Soon the two merged at the Morrilton location under the name of Harding College, so named after James A. Harding, a prominent Church of Christ pastor who had died in 1922. By 1934, the growing campus was overcrowded and bursting at its seams. Fortuitously, the Methodists had decided to close their very spacious women's only Galloway College in Searcy and merge it with Hendrix College in Conway. A subsequent offer to sell it to Harding for much less than it was worth was accepted quickly, and Harding College was in business in Searcy with the doors open for classes in the fall of 1934. The first instrumental group photo I could find was one from 1924 of the school's orchestra under the direction of faculty member Fannie Marie Moody. As for a true band on the campus, the first one was begun in the mid-1930s by a student at the school by the name of Robert Boyd, who directed the group during campus athletic contests and swing band events. But a campus band really took off in the early 1950s when Harding alumnus George Baggett returned to the campus and planted the seeds that established its future with his successors Warren Casey and the present director, Michael Chance. Currently the band program has about eighty members enrolled and the marching unit is known as the "Thunderin' Herd," obviously taken from the school's mascot, the Bison.

Among the interesting observations I made in my research of college and/or university bands in Arkansas was the fact that only three women have ever been in charge of a college band with both marching and concert components. They are Alma Brown (at Arkansas AM&N, now UAPB), Pat Brumbaugh (at ASU), and Sarah Mickey (at SAU).

What I have provided here is a synopsis of what is to follow in the chapters of this book. Each of the nine bands has its own chapter, and each chapter is meant to cover the general history of each school's band program with as much detail as reasonable space would allow.

In the researching and writing of this book, I have discovered facts and stories about which I never knew, confirmed a few I suspected or only thought I knew, and dispelled a number that were just gossip or simply blown out of proportion. But through all of it, I have had the time of my life. I have traveled a number of times to each of the campuses written about herein, met a host of most courteous and pleasantly helpful librarians, archivists, and other campus administrators and staff, and enjoyed the hospitality of numerous citizens in each of their respective communities. Many an hour has been spent going through college campus yearbooks, newspapers, curricula catalogs, and more than a few drawers of old photographs.

But most pleasant of all has been the visiting with current and former band directors of the "Arkansas College Nine" and current and former members of each band. This past year and a half I made a point of attending at least two football game performances of each school, catching basketball games when possible, and attending concert programs when performed in an attempt to not only catch the band members in action, but also to witness as much of their spirit as I could. For a Razorback fan of many years, it took some getting used to not expecting the Razorback Fight Song to be played after every score or during every timeout. As the song in the United Methodist hymnal relates,

> This is my home, the country where my heart is,
> here are my hopes, my dreams, my holy shrine;
> but other hearts in other lands are beating
> with hopes and dreams as true and high as mine.

You see, the University of Arkansas in Fayetteville is where my heart is, where my collegiate hopes and dreams took root, and is what some think is one of my shrines. But in my travels the scales fell from my eyes and I realized that there are other schools in my state that have similarly dedicated souls associated with their campuses "with hopes and dreams as true and high as mine."

I am truly impressed with the schools I have written about in this book and fully admire those who plug away each day, each month, and each year to continue making those campuses better for the students who matriculate there. And I follow that up with equal words of admiration for the band programs, their directors, student musicians, and alumni who present marching programs second to none, perform concerts with the keenest professionalism, and support the schools with an individualized spirit that places them in no one's shadow. I am taken aback by how hard that I have witnessed those collective 1,400+ student-musicians practice diligently for hour upon hour on their nine practice turfs to put on a show each week for the home crowd with nothing more tangible to show for it than one single semester's hour of credit. There has to be more of a reason for their tenacity and perseverance than just that. So, what is it? Look at their faces when they are performing, whether it is at a football field or in a concert setting, in a basketball field house or during a jazz band gig—it is in their faces. And when you see it, you will know. It's a band thing.

Moments that I will remember include hearing the fight songs of Henderson and Ouachita amazingly played to the tunes of the respective hymns of "Gimme That Old Time Religion" and "Will the Circle Be Unbroken?" Powerful stuff. And when the Tech Band stunned the American School Band Directors Association Convention in Hot Springs last summer, hands clapped so hard that they hurt. What a delight it was to see whole crowds of people show up at the final UAM football game of the season watching the band march and play while the team ended up with only a single victory by season's end. And it was impressive to watch how the crowds at Harding and SAU football games don't hit the concession stand when the buzzer goes off to signal the end of the first half—they stay to watch the band march! And the people in the stands applaud appreciatively at the end of the shows! And I'll never forget the ASU "War Party" pep band enjoying the heck out of the Lady Indians stomping the Lady Razorbacks in the Fowler Center during the NCAA Women's Basketball Tournament. A stunner that stopped me in my tracks was going to the UAPB–Southern football game in Pine Bluff and hearing the Golden Lion Band perform classic Sousa and other marches for almost thirty minutes in a pregame concert. Talking about destroying stereotypes! I also enjoyed attending the quarterfinal game of the Division IIA football championship playoff and watching the UCA Band cheer on the Bears only to suffer a heartbreaking loss.

But the thing I think that most genuinely impressed me about all the marching bands that I saw perform and concert bands that I heard play was the dedication of the students to the task at hand, regardless of the size of the crowd in the stands or in the audience. Whether the attendance was 100, or 1,000, or 10,000 or 25,000, the musicians played like they were performing in front of the whole state. And that reflects on a lesson they must have learned from their directors: namely, if it's worth doing at all, it is worth doing well. And that they did. I highly commend them all.

I would like to take a personal privilege here in highly recommending that you, the reader, take some time out and visit Arkansas's colleges and universities, regardless of whether they are large or small, public or private, two year or four year. If you don't already know the diversity of higher education that this state has to offer, you will be pleasantly surprised to discover how Arkansas's schools have improved over the years. And the same goes for the music programs on these campuses reflected in what the band programs are only a part. In addition to the band calendar, many of the choral, orchestral, and music education programs offered in this state are at the very least on par with many of those considered top-notch in other states. Concert programs running the musical gamut at all of the schools presented in this book, in addition to others not covered, are available on a regular basis and are some of the most affordable, uplifting, and rewarding entertainment values available today.

Finally, I would like to thank you for taking the time to read this book. It has been a joy to put together and an education I will always treasure. Should any errors show up, know that they are unintended and I apologize for them. And I realize that some of the photos included on these pages are not as sharply in focus as they probably should be. Where I could not find the original photos, I had to scan from yearbooks, and that resulted in third-generation pictures (this is also evident in photos scanned across two-page layouts). But my decision to include these images lay in the fact that I would rather have a less than perfect picture than none at all in telling these stories.

I would like for you to know that all profits from the sale of this book will go to support the Band Museum in Pine Bluff, Arkansas. If you haven't visited that bastion of band memorabilia, you have missed out on a real treat. Walls full of old instruments, historical photos of primary, secondary, and college bands, and an old-fashioned soda fountain await where you can sit and reminisce with old friends about band stories of yore. Find out more information about Jerry Horn's tribute to the legacy of all kinds of bands at bandmuseum.tripod.com and enjoy!

And now, without further ado, horns up!!

Chapter One

The Showband of Arkansas

Henderson State University
Henderson State College
Henderson State Teachers College
Henderson-Brown College
Henderson College
Arkadelphia Methodist College

The school known today as Hendrix College in Conway had as its forerunner the Altus Central Institute in Altus, Arkansas, built in 1876 by a Methodist minister, Reverend Isham L. Burrow. After changing its name to the Central Collegiate Institute in 1881 to elevate the school in the academic ranks, Burrow sold the campus in 1884 jointly to the Arkansas and Little Rock Methodist Conferences but remained as its president as he had been since the school's inception. He resigned his office three years later but stayed on at the institute as financial agent and professor emeritus. In 1889 the name of the school changed again to Hendrix College in honor of Bishop Eugene Hendrix, who presided over the two Arkansas conferences mentioned above. The following year, Hendrix moved to Conway.

When Hendrix officials started looking for a new location for the college, seven Arkansas towns made bids for the site. Conway was eventually chosen for the new campus because of its central location in the state, and the community leaders made good on their promise to clean up the town's seamier sides.

One of the towns that did not get the Hendrix bid was Arkadelphia. Holding firm in their interest in establishing a Methodist College in their midst, city leaders met with Little Rock Methodist Conference members less than a month after the Hendrix decision had been made. The citizens of Arkadelphia offered up land and a building to the Methodists if the church folks would start a coeducational college in their town. As stated in Nancy Britton's book, *Two Centuries of Methodism in Arkansas, 1800–2000,* the conference accepted the offer, "with the proviso that the curriculum of the Methodist college be equal to that of Ouachita Baptist College, already located in Arkadelphia." The school opened as Arkadelphia Methodist College in 1890 with 150 students and succeeded with notable academic success until it merged with Hendrix College in 1929.

Years before the merger, however, an ardent supporter by name of C. C. Henderson, who became the schools' board of trustees chairman, came forth with a sizable contribution, leading to the renaming of the school as Henderson College in 1904. And again in 1911 Henderson and a fellow admirer of the campus and fellow member of the board, W. W. Brown, each donated yet another financial sum, resulting in the school being designated Henderson-Brown College. But the Little Rock Methodist Conference officials decided that sponsoring these two colleges plus the one strictly for women at Galloway College in Searcy was too much for the state's denomination to support. So, the Henderson-Brown and Hendrix campuses were merged onto the Conway location and the Arkadelphia property was deeded back to the town's citizenry (also, the Galloway faculty and student body were eventually merged with those at Hendrix in 1933; see the Harding chapter of this book).

The Arkadelphia populace was still adamant about wanting a college at the old Henderson-Brown location and almost immediately approached the Arkansas General Assembly about accepting the campus as a debt-free gift to the state in exchange for the establishment of a teacher training school on its site. The offer was accepted and the school opened as Henderson State Teachers College in the fall of 1929 with most of the previous faculty and two-hundred-member student body still in place. As with most of the other colleges in the state at the time, there was a small preparatory school attached to HSTC.

In the 1903–04 Henderson Catalogue, along with other photos of campus life, there is the above left photo that is captioned, "College Orchestra 1903–04," apparently one of the earliest photographic records of an instrumental organization on the Arkadelphia campus, though a community brass band in Arkadelphia was formed as early as the 1870s according to John Gladden Hall, author of *Henderson State College: The Methodist Years, 1890–1929.* And as noted in the January 24, 1896, local weekly newspaper, the *Southern Standard,* the college orchestra played for the eleventh wedding anniversary party of the college's president and his wife, Dr. and Mrs. George C. Jones. In the 1904 *Star* yearbook there is the notation at the bottom of the page claiming that for the Music Department a "Full College Band will be maintained" with Professor Dwight Blake listed as its director. Just above the stage door frame (*in the above right photo*) is a sign that says 1906 Henderson Orchestra.

In the 1907 *Star* yearbook, the above photo of the Henderson College sophomore class was printed. As with other Arkansas colleges of the period, there was a military contingent on the campus that included all male enrollees of the school as reflected in the uniforms on the men in the picture. The women's dress was uniform also, though their requisite participation in the military program only existed for that single year; their wearing of the attire on campus, however, was required for the next few terms.

According to Dr. John G. Hall, intramural sports began on the Henderson campus as early as 1896. But intercollegiate play didn't start until 1904 with baseball and the following year for track and football; basketball competition began in 1920.

Above left is a 1909 photo showing the Henderson Band in the bleachers at right viewing a sporting event in the partially constructed grandstand on campus. The pose above right was made of the Henderson College Band in 1910 with Dwight Blake (*seated front row left*) still listed as the men's director. The photo below is of the Henderson-Brown cadet brigade on parade on the grounds in front of the campus's Old Main building in 1911 (the school added the Brown portion of its name that year). Unfortunately, the structure burned down in 1914.

In addition to the Henderson-Brown Band shown above for the 1910–11 school year, there was also a photo in the *Star* yearbook of the school's orchestra (*above right*). The college's military band of 1911–12 is shown below right along with what the *Star* yearbook described as "Dr. Crowell's Ragtime Band," pictured below left. Note that Professor Dwight Blake's posture was almost identical in both photos. By 1919 the school had adopted as its motto "The School With a Heart In It," according to Dr. John G. Hall. Later it would be modified to "The School With a Heart."

There is no further documentation in the school files of a band on the campus of Henderson-Brown until 1928, but photos do exist of the campus orchestra. In fact, in 1913 Frederick A. Harwood became the school's new head of the music conservatory, serving as the orchestra conductor for many years (he retired from Henderson in 1946). Above are photos from 1915–16 (*top left*) and 1918–19 and below are ones from 1921–22 (*left*) and 1923–24 (*right*).

The last documentation of a band at Henderson-Brown prior to the school being merged with Hendrix College in Conway was the above arrangement of individual band members' photos in the 1928 *Star* yearbook with James A. Tull (*bottom row center*) listed as the group's director. After the campus reverted back to the city of Arkadelphia in 1929 and the state of Arkansas agreed to open a teachers' college within the facilities in the fall of that year, a band once again appeared at the school in 1930–31 with T. J. Ashford as conductor. The photos below are from *Star* yearbooks taken on the steps of the Henderson State Teachers College main building with Professor T. J. Ashford holding the director's baton standing in the left front row and wearing sunshades in both pictures. Note that Ashford had been legally blind from birth. The student listing under the 1933–34 band photo at left identified Hugh Patterson and Jack Watson as drum majors (*extreme left and right front row, respectively*), and the caption under the 1934–35 photo at right called the group the Henderson Reddie Band. The school had adopted the "Reddie" mascot in the 1920s.

The 1935–36 Henderson State Teachers College Band is shown above on the field of Ouachita Baptist College's football field during one of the schools' annual rival meetings on the gridiron. Note in the photo at right the band forming an "H" on the turf (a formation also native to Hendrix College and Harding College at the time). The photo in the middle is of the Homecoming court and cheerleaders for 1935. The bottom left photo is of the 1936–37 HSTC Band with J. O. Burns and Lois Ashford (*extreme left and right front row, respectively*) serving as drum majors. The bottom right photo below records the band's participation during the Homecoming Parade of 1936.

T. J. Ashford
Director

A Reserve Officer Training Corps unit was established on the HSTC campus in 1936 to prepare students for leadership roles in the military after graduation from college. As part of that program, the ROTC Band, separate from the college band, took its place on campus. Above is the 1938–39 HSTC Marching Band on the football field during halftime break in a game and on parade through the Arkadelphia streets. Also shown above is a copy of the school's complete alma mater as printed in the 1939 *Star* yearbook. Below is the 1939–40 HSTC Band going through their paces on the school's football field and that year's ROTC Band fronted by drum major cadet Reynolds and commanded by a Second Lieutenant English.

As the United States came closer to eventual entry into World War II, the HSTC Marching Band and the ROTC Band merged into one unit as young men from the campus began entering the military branches for service. The snapshots above are of the 1940–41 HSTC Band, while the photos below show the band in the fall of 1941 playing at a football game in their military band uniforms and in a yearbook pose on the field.

The 1942–43 HSTC Band is shown in the above photo led by student commander Thomas B. Walker (*inset*) with its director listed simply as Sergeant Sheets and the drum major as Private Oliver. That year also saw the appearance on campus of the Collegians dance band shown below left. Also on parade the following year was the small HSTC Aviation Cadet Band in the lower right photo.

Millard Laing

With World War II over in the summer of 1945 HSTC experienced what most college campuses did for the next few years with thousands of military men returning to get their degrees via the GI Bill. The HSTC Band also regained members in its ranks with an increase in both men and women musicians. Above is the 1946–47 HSTC Band playing in the school's football stands still wearing the military uniforms from before and the Concert Band at right under the direction of student Millard M. Laing. For 1947–48 Glen Riggin was hired as the new faculty member to direct the band (shown below with that year's Concert Band) while Laing played an instrument in the group. During the season, the band wore white overalls in lieu of the old military uniforms as seen below.

Once again, after the war the HSTC Marching Band and the ROTC Battalion Band became separate groups as reflected in the 1948–49 photos above. The drum major for the HSTC Band that year was Clem Carolan shown above left. Below are the Marching and Concert Bands and their trumpeters for the 1949–50 school year.

During the 1950–51 school year the Collegians dance band played frequently for on-campus dances (the circular inset is of Joe Wood, band president). For that year's football team, the HSTC Marching Band played for each home game and featured drum major Bob Smith and the two male twirlers, Tinky Ault and R. L. Bryant, pictured above. Below is band director Glen W. Riggin and the 1951–52 HSTC majorette line.

Glen W. Riggin
Band Director

The photos above record drum major R. L. Bryant and the 1952–53 HSTC majorettes along with the Concert Band for that year dressed up in gowns and suits prior to a spring concert. And below are the HSTC Concert and Marching Bands for 1953–54, along with a photo of that year's director, Robert Hardesty.

Though the photo above only shows about twenty-six members belonging to the 1954–55 HSTC Marching Band, the *Star* yearbook lists more like fifty by name in the group. Harold Mitchell (*front row right*) served as drum major for the years 1954–56. Also above is the smaller by-audition-only Concert Band directed by Robert Hardesty that presented several "pops" concerts, open-air concerts, and regular formal concerts on campus; the group also went on a concert tour during the school year. Orville Kelley was the new director for the 1955–56 HSTC Bands as well as for the Collegians dance band. Below are both the Marching Reddies and the ROTC Band for that school year period.

For 1956–57 the HSTC Reddie Band received new maroon and oxford gray uniforms as worn in marching and concert settings shown above. Also pictured is director Orville Kelley, a Henderson alumnus. Below is the Collegians dance band for 1956–57 that played for out of town gigs as well as for dances on the school campus. Also below is the 1957–58 ROTC Band commanded by Cadet Jack Gordon, who also happened to play in the Reddie Marching and Concert Bands as well as with the Collegians.

Beginning with the 1958 fall semester Wendell O. Evanson began his long association with the HSTC band program as its Director of Bands. He is shown above (*in dark suit*) fronting the Collegians dance band. Also shown are the majorettes for the 1958–59 marching season. Below is the Concert Band for 1959–60 of which the *Star* yearbook mentioned that two-thirds of the band members were on scholarship. Also pictured is drum major Ronnie Inzer.

Wendell O. Evanson

The 1960–61 Reddie Band numbered forty-three on its roster and is shown above in a concert arrangement. Drum major for that year was Connie Harvey, seated with a baritone wearing a white jacket to the right in the above photo. Also in May of 1960 the Collegians dance band (*above left*) traveled to Honolulu, Tokyo, Okinawa, and Iwo Jima on a tour sponsored by the USO to entertain U.S. service personnel stationed abroad. The trip lasted five weeks, ending July 3 back home. Ronnie Formby (*standing in center of lower right photo*) served as drum major for the forty-eight-member 1961–62 ASTC Band. The band had the pleasure of marching in the Mardi Gras Parade in New Orleans each of the years represented on this page.

The 1962–63 Henderson Marching Band is shown above, fronted on the home field by drum major Judy Stephenson and in the stands directed by Wendell Evanson (*in raincoat down front*) during the final football game of the season against the ASTC Bears. That game, played in Searcy, was cold and wet, and as the 1963 *Star* yearbook described it, "the (HSTC) marching band sloshed and splashed through their halftime performance." The 1963–64 Reddie Concert Band is shown below along with the HSTC Band marching in the 1963 Homecoming Parade in Arkadelphia.

For the 1964–65 HSTC marching season, Ginny Pace (*above right*) served as the group's drum major. Also shown are that season's Concert Band and the renowned Collegians, "considered one of the finest stage bands in the nation" (quoted from the 1965 *Star* yearbook). Very popular with the USO, the Collegians, directed by Wendell Evanson, toured bases in the Caribbean during the summer of 1965. The string bass player was Hal Cooper, who later became the director of the Arkansas Tech Bands (and still is as of this writing). Below is the 1965–66 Reddie Band marching in the 1965 Homecoming Parade led by drum major Joe Ed Gunn.

For the 1966–67 school year the Reddie Marching Band (*above left*) traveled to Southern State College in Magnolia and Arkansas A&M in Monticello in support of the football team as well as performing at all home games and on-campus pep rallies (*above right*). Consistent with previous and subsequent years, director Evanson's students proudly represented HSC in the Arkansas Intercollegiate Band in January 1967, with eighteen of his fifty-six musicians being so honored. Note that the college dropped the "Teachers" portion of its name in 1967; it was known as Henderson State College for the next few years. Below are the Reddie majorette line and Concert Band for 1967–68.

By the 1968–69 school year the Reddie Marching Band had been dubbed "The Pride of Henderson." The Concert Band (*shown above*) was equally proud of its presentations performed in the on-campus Arkansas Hall and of its director, Wendell Evanson, having the school's yearbook, the *Star,* dedicated in his honor for 1969. Below, the band's majorettes for the 1969–70 season flank drum major Lee Finch and the Brass Ensemble poses for a yearbook photograph.

Beginning with the 1970–71 football season the Henderson State College Marching Band shown above called itself the "Showband of Arkansas." Also on display above are the drum major and twirlers for that year's band. The school's stage band was at the time called the Jazz Rock Stage Band and was under the direction of Earl Hesse. The HSC Symphonic Band for 1971–72 is shown below as are members of that year's Brass Quintet. The seventy-two-member Symphonic Band was one of only five collegiate bands to perform at the College Band Directors National Association's Southwest Regional Convention in Manhattan, Kansas. George Sparks was the drum major for that year.

And at Halftime . . .

The ninety-member 1972–73 Henderson Reddie Marching Band steps onto the field for yet another expected stellar halftime appearance. Later in that school year the Symphonic Band performed at the MENC Regional Convention in Wichita, Kansas. At the time, in addition to Wendell Evanson serving as HSC's Director of Bands, the music faculty also included Earl Hesse and David Ettienne as woodwind instructors and Don Kramer and Wayne Harrison as brass instructors. For 1973–74 the Reddie Band added a new flag line to the flash and dash of the group's already established panache, joining the glitter of the majorette line below and the audio and video impact of the tuba section.

Henderson State College became Henderson State University in 1974 involving yet another change in campus stationery. During the 1974–75 marching season, Earl Hesse assisted Wendell Evanson in directing the eighty-six-member Reddie Marching Band and continued directing the campus stage band as shown above left. Below, the 1975–76 Reddie Marching Band and the Stage Band are shown. In April 1976, the HSU, Ouachita Baptist University, and Arkadelphia bands and choirs joined together in a Bicentennial salute to America at Haygood Stadium on the HSU campus. OBU composer-in-residence Dr. Francis McBeth wrote a special composition that was performed at the event.

The uniforms that the HSU Reddie Band wore in the 1976–77 season shown above were replaced with new bolero-bloused tops in 1977–78 as seen in the photos below. The Symphonic Band is also pictured below in the spring of 1978 performing for end-of-the-year graduation ceremonies.

HSU's "Showband of Arkansas" displayed the twirling talents of Greg Burton during the 1977, 1978, and 1979 marching seasons with his airborne objects of choice including multiple regular batons, fire batons, and even knives. The 1978–79 marching band included ninety members led on the field by drum major Kent McAnally. Also shown above are that year's Concert Band and members of one of the two Jazz Bands on campus. The latter were directed by Earl Hesse (Jazz Band 1) and Wes Branstine (Jazz Band 2). Below are photos of the 1979–80 Marching Reddie Band on the field and in the stands in Haygood Stadium and the Concert Band in performance on campus in Arkansas Hall.

When the Henderson Reddie Marching Band (*above*) took to the field in 1980–81, they did so under the leadership of drum major Ed Grissom. That season saw a number of half-time solos performed by trumpeter Tom Strait (*above right*). And, as they had for many seasons before, the school's two Jazz Bands alternated playing for on-campus basketball games, conjuring up "That Old Reddie Spirit." But for 1981–82 another group within the Music Department, the Reddie Court Jesters (*pictured below*), was formed to play at basketball games under the direction of faculty member Dr. Doug Demorrow. Also shown below are members of the 1981–82 Marching Reddie brass section playing to the cheap seats and that season's Concert Band performing another spring selection. Jay Wilkins served as the band's drum major in 1981–82.

The 1982–83 edition of Henderson's "Showband" took to the marching field with over one hundred members in its ranks as seen above, including the rifle squad shown above right. Below is displayed the 1983–84 Marching Reddie Band playing both from the stands and from the field in formation. Doug Camp served as drum major.

The Henderson Reddie Band continued to grow in numbers for the school year 1984–85 as evidenced in the above photo as the unit goes through its paces during a half-time show. Beth Macchiarolo was drum major for the group that year. Also on view above is Jazz Band I directed by Dr. Wesley Branstine (*second from right, back row*). HSU band director Wendell Evanson is shown below watching the Homecoming game from the Haygood Stadium bleachers in the fall of 1985. His student musicians are also shown below rehearsing with the Flag Corps going through a routine on the field and the keyboard players practicing in the pit.

The 1986–87 Marching Reddie Band is shown above participating in the Clark County Fair Parade as is the HSU Flag Line. Also shown is twirler Leslie Branstine. Drum major for the 113-member organization was Monty Hill. Below is the 1987–88 HSU Band playing for an on-campus pep rally and performing at a Reddie football game in Haygood Stadium. The 1987–88 school year was Wendell Evanson's last year as Director of Bands at HSU—he officially retired at the end of the spring term after having spent thirty years atop the Reddie podium.

David Rollins accepted the honor of succeeding Wendell Evanson as the new Director of Bands at HSU for 1988–89. Hitting the ground running, Rollins, along with assistant band director and percussion instructor Rick Dimond, designed a color-coded system for learning marching routines, and his 120-member Marching Reddies joined for the ride. David Bretz served as drum major for the group shown above. Also pictured is part of the Reddie Brass playing at a home basketball game.

One of the most public events of the 1989–90 HSU school year was the Centennial Concert held in Arkansas Hall on March 8 celebrating one hundred years of a college being in existence on the campus (it started out as Arkadelphia Methodist College in 1890; refer back to earlier parts of this chapter for the various changes in the school's name and private/public school status). Shown below are HSU's charter members of the Kappa Kappa Psi and Tau Beta Sigma chapters of the national band service fraternity and sorority, respectively. Also shown are members of the Reddie Band performing for Parents' Day activities outside the Caddo Cafeteria.

The most groundbreaking event for the 1990–91 Reddie Band was the most literal one. Work began on the construction of the new Garrison Center on campus, which included the 5,000-square-foot Evanson Band Hall (named after former band director Wendell Evanson) where the HSU Concert Band is shown above in its inaugural performance during the Christmas Concert. Also shown is that year's Marching Reddie Band with drum major Amy Bucher. Drum major Brandon Brewer (*below*) readies the 1991–92 HSU Band to play the Reddie Spirit Fight Song as the group stands atop the ridge above Carpenter-Haygood Stadium before a football game. Also below, a portion of the 110 members of the Symphonic Band who participated in a three-state Spring Concert Tour listen to a performance critique by director David Rollins.

The above two photos show 1992–93 Marching Reddie Band members playing both in the stands and performing on the field. Pit and auxiliary groups such as the flags added more audio and video flair to the band's halftime shows and became more important to the overall presentations as the years progressed. Below is the 1993–94 HSU Band flanked on the left by director David Rollins and feature twirler Robin Fannin and on the right by drum major Brian Henry.

Pictured above are the HSU Symphonic Band and the HSU Concert Band for 1994–95, while the school's 1995–96 "Showband" is shown below in a performance setting during the 1995 Homecoming halftime show and a photo sitting for the 1996 *Star* yearbook. Jeff Coventry served as drum major for the latter group. Also about this time, the phrase "Eat More Spam" enters the band's lexicon (ask a Reddie Band member about that one).

For the 1996–97 school year the Marching Reddie Band boasted having 140+ members in its ranks and produced halftime shows that included special arrangements of "On Broadway," "McArthur Park," and "Malaga" directed on the field by drum major Chris Moix. Also above, Reddie Band members are shown crowding into the ravine separating HSU and OBU, during the "Battle of the Ravine" pep rally before the Henderson-Ouachita football game. Below, from the top ledge of Carpenter-Haygood Stadium, the 1997–98 Reddie Band plays the traditional "B Flat to G" prior to a home game and marches down Arkadelphia's Main Street during the city's annual Christmas Parade.

The above 1998–99 Marching Reddie Band took to the field counting 164 members in its rank-and-file led by drum major Stephen Moss. David Rollins, Director of Bands, is shown to the extreme left in the group photo. Popular halftime themes for the band were "Tower of Power" and "Bond, that's James Bond." Developed over the years, the highlight marching event of the season came to be the "Battle of the Bands" when Henderson played Arkansas Tech (that year in Russellville). Augmenting the Reddie sound that year was the addition of electric guitar and bass played by Shawn Keeter and Daniel Schoultz, respectively. Below are group photos of the band's chapters of Tau Beta Sigma sorority and Kappa Kappa Psi fraternity for the school year 1999–2000.

One of the halftime shows the 2000–2001 Marching Reddie Band performed was one based on the music from the musical *Tommy*. In addition to marching at the regularly scheduled HSU football games, the Henderson Band (*shown above*) also participated in a number of marching contests performing exhibitions in Texas and Arkansas. In the spring the Symphonic Band toured neighboring cities and towns performing for high school audiences and also sitting in with high school bands to help the musicians to improve their skills. Henderson's 2001–02 edition of "The Showband of Arkansas" is pictured below performing before a Carpenter-Haygood Stadium audience and playing on "the hill" prior to the kickoff of another home football game. Zach McClung was drum major for the marching seasons 2000–2002.

David Rollins
Assistant Prof. of Music /
Director of Bands

Once again the HSU Marching Reddie Band in 2002–03 (*pictured above*) topped out over 140 members with director David Rollins. The other two photos above from that season show the Reddie Pep Band at a campus pep rally and a marimba player performing in the pit during a halftime presentation. Below is HSU drum major Adam McFarlin (he served in that role for three years, 2003–05) with the 2003–04 Showband of Arkansas and more Pep Band members playing at yet another pep rally in the fall of 2003.

The portraits of the Henderson Reddie Band on this page are of the marching units of the 2004 and 2005 groups, above and below respectively, that support the school's athletic intercollegiate program in the Division II Gulf South Conference. Perhaps the biggest news for the band in years occurred with the announcement by David Rollins prior to the 2005 marching season that the 2005–06 school year would be his last as Director of Bands at Henderson State University. Following an extensive search and interview process, the school filled the position beginning in the summer of 2006 with Jesse Leyva, who was in the process of completing his Doctor of Musical Arts degree at Arizona State University after having taught in public and private secondary education and on the collegiate level in California.

As of this printing, Henderson State University offers degree programs to instrumental performers culminating with either a Bachelor of Arts in Music or a Bachelor of Music, with the latter denoting a specialization in performance, composition, or education.

Chapter Two

Marching Bears
The Sound of Central Arkansas

University of Central Arkansas
State College of Arkansas
Arkansas State Teachers College
Arkansas State Normal School

THE NORMAL BAND

When the school known today as the University of Central Arkansas was created by the Arkansas General Assembly in 1907, it was called Arkansas State Normal School and was established in Conway for the purpose of training students to become primary and secondary teachers in the state. "Normal" was the term used at the time to refer to a teaching school. The first pictorial evidence of an instrumental organization on the campus was the above photo from the 1915 *Scroll* yearbook—note the title of the band: "The Normal Band." Unlike some Arkansas schools, women were members from day one. The director of the group was listed as John T. Buchholz, standing to the extreme left in the photo holding a baton. Buchholz was also named as the director in the yearbook the following year and is standing in the front row, fourth from the left, in the photo below.

The next photo of a band on the Arkansas State Normal campus was the one above from the 1917 yearbook with the caption, "Band Practice." In the photo the students on the steps of the left entry to the main campus building are apparently rehearsing outside and entertaining the larger group of students congregating around the steps of the right entry. No photos of a campus band were listed among the pages of either the 1918 or 1919 year-books. For the 1919–20 school year the students below posed on the steps of the building shown above for their annual yearbook photo session. The new band director was listed as Homer F. Hess (*third from left, on the second row, with hair parted in middle*), and there is a sudden absence of women in the organization.

The photo above of the Arkansas State Normal Band was printed in the 1921 *Scroll* yearbook while the two below of the 1921–22 band and orchestra were printed in the subsequent yearbook. The following paragraphs accompanied the photos below:

> The Normal School Band was almost entirely reorganized at the beginning of the school year on account of the large number of men who were members of the band last year who failed to return to school this year. Prof. Homer F. Hess, Director, determined to run the organization on a different basis this year to what it had ever been run before. To that end a course in direction of school bands was inaugurated in connection with the regular practice nights which are held at the school twice each week. Schools are asking the Normal School to send teachers who can direct a band, but under the old course of pure instrumental music, members of the band were not capable of undertaking the direction of a band . . .
>
> Last year Mr. Hess came to the conclusion that he could not expect a sufficient number of violin students to enter school annually to keep up (the orchestra), so he offered a beginners course in violin free to all students at the beginning of the school year. His invitation was accepted by a large number of students, many of them showing talent and being admitted to membership in the orchestra.

The caption under the photo above from the 1923 *Scroll* yearbook mentioned that the band made several appearances during the school year and apparently improved with each performance. Also, the following sentence was included: "New instruments which were given the organization by the school, have added materially to the quality of music rendered." The band showed a loss of members in the group's photo (*below*) in the 1924 *Scroll,* and there is no further mention of a campus band until its reappearance in the 1931 yearbook. Homer Hess, the director of the band and the orchestra, was also listed in 1924 as being the "Head of Conservatory."

Homer F. Hess
Head of Conservatory

For the 1924–25 school year the above group performed as the orchestra for Arkansas State Teachers College—the school's name was officially changed in early 1925. Homer Hess was still the conductor of the orchestra, but no band was mentioned in the yearbook. It was reported that the above group broadcast a program over radio from Hot Springs in February and performed at the spring festival in Conway. The next mention of the orchestra occurred in 1929 with the group being listed in that year's *Scroll* as being under the direction of L. C. Thompson, the tall man wearing a bow tie in the center of the back row in the photo below.

For the 1929–30 school term Homer Hess is once again listed in the yearbook as being the director of the ASTC Orchestra pictured above. And in the following year's book, the band makes its first appearance in the *Scroll* since 1924. The two photos below from the 1931 *Scroll* illustrate the band's appearance on the sidelines during the 1930 Homecoming game and in the gymnasium in front of a number of the student body during a break at a campus dance.

Over the next few years the ASTC Band would be under the direction of a number of different men, as the baton was passed on often. For 1935–36 J. D. (John) Henley directed the group and is shown in the above picture at left holding a baton. Notice that women are once again in the picture. The yearbook stated that the band played at all home football games and "accompanied the Bears to Russellville for their battle with the 'Wonder Boys.'" During concert season the group presented a number of on-campus concerts and one in Morrilton. By 1937 the head of the college's music department, Homer Hess, was back for another stint as the band director, leading the group as it performed at on-campus and a couple of away football games and on-campus basketball games. In between games the ASTC Band also presented a series of on-campus concerts. The photo below is from the 1938 *Scroll.*

J. H. Branchcomb
Director

    The 1938–39 ASTC Band had a new director in J. H. Branchcomb, a new drum major in Charles R. Turner, and new uniforms all around. They also had a new instrumental group on campus—the "Tophatters" dance orchestra shown at top along with the ASTC Band on the sidelines showing off their new look. For 1940–41 the leadership changed again with John L. Adams directing the ASTC Band for the year. He is shown at left in the photo below. In the spring of both 1939 and 1940, the ASTC Band accepted invitations to perform at the Cotton Carnival in Memphis.

Paul Cooper

Paul Cooper started off the 1940–41 school year as the next ASTC Band director, but before the term was over he had to leave the position due to his National Guard Unit being mobilized. Music Department head Homer Hess completed the year, assisted by several student directors. Shown above is the band during concert season and the band marching during the Homecoming Parade. Andrew Mikita took over the baton for the 1941–42 season even though many men left the ASTC Band before the end of the year to serve in the military after the bombing of Pearl Harbor. The photo below of the band that year was taken during the fall term when the band was still at full strength. The second photo shows the band playing for a pep rally prior to a football game.

Andrew Mikita
Director

Milton Trusler
Director

After a number of years of single-year or less-than-single-year directors, the ASTC Band finally held on to one for a while with Milton Trusler, who joined the college faculty in 1942. His 1942–43 band is shown on the stage of the campus auditorium in the above photo. He also directed the "Tophatters" dance orchestra shown below in a 1944 photo. But the latter group was so depleted of players due to the war that two musicians from nearby Hendrix College and two more from Conway High School had to be recruited to round out the sound.

Even though World War II ended in the summer of 1945, the ASTC Band took a while to recover in terms of the number of students in its ranks. The above photo is of the 1944–45 band of which only four of the twenty-one members were male. By the following year, enrollment was up somewhat with thirty students listed by name in the 1945–46 *Scroll* under the photo below. Milton Trusler was still band director at the time.

The photo above records the drum major and her three majorettes leading a column of ASTC Band members onto the field for a halftime performance at a football game on campus in the fall of 1946. The yearbook listed thirty-seven students as making up the unit that year. Even though there are only thirty-nine members of the 1947–48 ASTC Band shown in the photo below, the *Scroll* that year noted that by the end of the year fifty-eight musicians were playing in the organization. The drum major that year was J. P. Crumpler (seated in white uniform at right) and the majorettes listed were Marvine Reynolds, Maxie Mae Elder, Anna Callan, M. Alice Linder, and Billie Jean Holland. Besides the expected football appearances, the band also performed a series of concerts at high schools in Wynne, Searcy, Newport, Forrest City, Alma, Van Buren, and Conway and in a joint concert with Hendrix College and Conway High School bands in April.

Despite their being grainy, the photos of the 1948–49 ASTC Band marching in the 1948 Homecoming Parade and practicing for a spring concert show the group hard at work. The third photo is of the "Tophatters" back in full form after the war. The 1949–50 school year was Milton Trusler's last year as director of the ASTC Band program. Shown at the extreme left in the back row below with his fifty- to sixty-member band, Trusler is credited with keeping the program intact through the war years and bringing it back from near extinction on campus.

The photo above left records the ASTC Band marching in the 1950 Homecoming Parade led by the drum major and five short-skirted majorettes, while the above right photo shows a few band members taking part in a jam session. During the early to mid-1950s the ASTC Band was led by Herbert Haskett, who had been the band's assistant director under Milton Trusler. Haskett is standing to the left in the 1951–52 picture below.

The above photo shows the 1952–53 ASTC Band posing in front of the newly completed Music Building on campus. The new facility afforded the entire music program more practice areas in which to rehearse and storage space for instruments and music. Drum major John Hall is also pictured above with the five-woman majorette line that performed during the year. Below a few ASTC Band members are shown marching in the 1953 Homecoming Parade along with the "Tophatters" from a 1954 *Scroll* yearbook photo.

The 1954–55 ASTC Marching Band is shown in the photo above wearing new uniforms they received in time for football season. That season John Hall served his third year as the group's drum major (he later became a history professor on the Henderson campus and author of *Henderson State College: The Methodist Years, 1890–1929*, referenced in this book's chapter on HSU). Also shown is the school's resurrected orchestra with the College Choir. Below, the 1955–56 ASTC Band peers at the camera from the sidelines during the 1955 Homecoming game.

Dr. Victor Hardt (*at right*) signed on with ASTC as the new band director for the 1956–57 school year. With his doctorate from Columbia University in New York City, he directed the students pictured above, who were led on the field by Helen Owen Hendrixson, posed at the extreme right in the twirlers' photo. New to the band's repertoire in 1957 was the creation of a drill team consisting of twenty-four women called the "T-Steppers." At times they would march with the band as in the photo below and at others they would perform solo routines similar to the Kilgore Rangerettes. The band's drum major for 1957–58 was Syble Owen.

Homer Brown began his long tenure as the director of the ASTC Band in the fall of 1958 directing the musicians above standing on risers for a 1959 *Scroll* photo session. As noted in the yearbook: "The ASTC Band, our band, was a great morale booster and raised the volume on our School Spirit." The other photo above was taken as the band marched through downtown Conway during the 1958 Homecoming Parade. The photo of the home football stadium below in the fall of 1960 shows the crowd standing with the ASTC Band out of respect for the American flag being presented during pregame ceremonies.

Homer Brown
Director

Those who marched in front of the 1960–61 ASTC Marching Band were drum major Ray Jackson, feature twirlers Sandra De Long and Linda Foshee, and the six-woman majorette line shown above. Also pictured is the Pep Band that provided music for the home basketball games. Below, Homer Brown directs the 1961–62 ASTC Band during a rehearsal in the Music Building's band room, and the group led by drum major Robin Nix marches in the 1961 Homecoming Parade. The yearbook indicated that there were sixty-four members in the band that year and that one of the highlights for the group was the Spring Tour of high schools in southwest Arkansas.

David Ritter
Associate Director

Joining Homer Brown on the ASTC Band staff for 1962–63 was David Ritter as associate director. Shown also is that year's band in concert formation and in action playing for a pep rally held in the circle in front of the campus's main building. The 1963–64 ASTC Band was one of the Arkansas college bands that played for the dedication of the new Heber Springs Dam when President John Kennedy was there just six weeks before he was assassinated. Below are the "Tophatters" stage band and newly formed Brass Choir, both directed by David Ritter.

Perhaps one of the most exciting events if not the most exciting event for the 1964–65 ASTC Band was marching in the January 20, 1965, Presidential Inaugural Parade of Lyndon Johnson in Washington, D.C., as pictured above. Johnson and Vice President Humphrey and their wives are seated in the reviewing stands above watching the band pass in review. For 1965–66 Homer Brown took on a new assistant in Pat Hasty, who also took over as director of the Brass Choir and "Tophatters" (Hasty is standing at left in both photos below). Note the band wearing new uniforms below, with dress coats worn over either skirts or pants for concert wear. During marching season all rank-and-file members wore pants with the coat and an additional overlay vest and cap.

The 1966–67 Marching Bears included the seven majorettes shown above along with three feature twirlers. The new uniforms for the rest of the marching band can be seen at right as the Concert Band poses in their concert attire. The year 1967 was also the year that ASTC had its name changed to State College of Arkansas; more familiarly, SCA. Homer Brown is shown below directing the 1967–68 Marching Bears at a home football game and again later that school year in the band room facilities in the new Fine Arts Center, which was dedicated on February 25. The band, along with the SCA Choir and Little Symphony (made up of SCA students, faculty, and townspeople), performed for the ceremonies.

The 1968–69 SCA Marching Bears can be seen above on the campus football field being led by drum major Bill Phelps in playing a march. Pat Hasty is also shown above with the Brass Choir, having a great time during their *Scroll* yearbook photo session. The formation shown below shows the 1969–70 SCA Band spell out the college's recently acquired new monogram on the field surrounded by the newly formed "Stepperettes" drill team. Also shown is a ground view of the band performing at a halftime show that fall.

The SCA Band shown above was one of the Arkansas college bands invited to march in Dale Bumpers's inaugural parade after he was sworn in as the new governor of Arkansas in January 1971. With Pat Hasty taking on other duties in the Music Department, Donald Fox joined the band staff as Homer Brown's new assistant director for 1970–71. Also shown above is the Concert Band playing its annual Christmas Concert in December 1970. Beginning in the fall of 1971, the SCA Band added some more variety and color to its ranks with a new flag corps present in the photo below. According to the *Scroll* yearbook the band had grown to ninety-eight members. The second photo below shows the Concert Band performing in Ida Waldran Auditorium on campus.

The photo above left showcases the 1972–73 SCA Band posing in the stands of Estes Stadium on campus. Among the smaller ensemble groups within the band that also performed in programs and concerts throughout the state was the Saxophone Ensemble (*above right*), which included director Homer Brown (*standing at left in the photo*). The longest trip the band made in 1973 was to Washington, D.C., to march in the second inaugural parade of President Richard Nixon on January 20. The SCA Marching Bears led by drum major David Finch was the thirty-sixth unit in the parade. The photos below were taken of the SCA Band during the 1973 Homecoming Parade as the group marched through the streets of Conway.

With the 1974–75 Marching Bears outfitted in their brand-new uniforms, including shako hats, their appearance in the Faulkner County Fair Parade above made quite a splash. The group, led by drum major Ricky Goode (*above*), also marched in the Pine Bluff and Harrison Christmas Parades as well as the SCA Homecoming Parade in 1974. Lee Hinson, drum major for the 1975–76 UCA Band, sits down front as the group poses in Estes Stadium for the lower right photo. (Note SCA became the University of Central Arkansas in 1975 as reflected in the uniforms.) The Marching Bears (a.k.a. "Homer's Heroes") are shown in the lower left photo displaying their school spirit at the Ouachita game in 1975.

Whereas the previous season had seen the UCA Band march to shows with a "Bicentennial" theme, the 1976–77 season was focused on supporting the football team in its quest for the AIC Championship, which it won, and the ensuing NAIA postseason play-offs. The team made it to the finals of the NAIA Champions Bowl game where they played Texas A&I at Kingsville, Texas, broadcast over television. The above left photo shows an image of the band and the Stepperettes in a photo taken from a television screen during the game. The bottom two photos show drum major Lee Hinson with the 1977–78 UCA Twirlers and a shot of that fall's band in Estes Stadium with the Stepperettes awaiting their turn on the sidelines.

Homer Brown, MME
Assistant Professor
Director of Bands

Pat Hasty, MM
Assistant Professor
Assistant Director of Bands

The 1978–79 school year was the last year that Homer Brown served as band director of the Marching Bears and the Concert Band. His assistant again that year was Pat Hasty. The auxiliary units serving the band that year are shown in the top photo, while the rank-and-file members are pictured above right marching in the 1978 Homecoming Parade. Russell Langston, with his Master's degree in Music Education, became the new Director of Bands in 1979–80 (Langston had also spent his undergraduate years studying at Arkansas Tech). Guest soloists with the band during halftime shows and concert presentations included Don Sheffield from Nashville and Arkansas's governor Bill Clinton.

R. Langston, M.Ed
Director of Bands

On the UCA campus in 1980–81 in addition to the Marching Bears and the Concert Band, the band program included a Jazz Ensemble (*shown above left*) and a Dixieland Band. At right above is pictured the Silas D. Snow Fine Arts Center where the band rehearsal hall, practice rooms, and offices are housed. Below is the percussion section during a halftime performance and the 150-member 1981–82 UCA Marching Band led by drum major Brian Fowlkes. Take note of the band's new uniforms.

The photo above depicts former UCA band director Homer Brown directing the UCA Alumni Band during the 1982 Homecoming game in Estes Stadium. His former band students would forever be known as "Homer's Heroes." Also shown above is a photo of the UCA Jazz Ensemble performing at the faculty Christmas party in December 1982. Members of the 1983–84 UCA Marching Bears below pose in front of the main building on campus, 136-members strong and led by drum major Paul Hawkins.

The 1984–85 edition of the Marching Bears is pictured above in this on-campus shot fronted by a flag line, a rifle team, twirlers, and Paul Hawkins as drum major. Also shown is the campus Kappa Kappa Psi fraternity (Epsilon Beta chapter) that served the band that year. Below the 1985–86 UCA Band is shown during an evening rehearsal in Estes Stadium preparing for an upcoming halftime show. Members of the year's Tau Beta Sigma Band sorority are shown sitting on the steps of the Snow Fine Arts Center.

In what became a familiar band pose for the *Scroll* yearbooks, the 1986–87 UCA Band took its turn on the steps shown above and had this shot taken. Brady Massey was the group's drum major and Shari Primm, Rhonda Hawkins, and Natalie Fox were the twirlers. As was a frequent occurrence in the 1980s, the 1987 Homecoming festivities were fairly damp, though the rain held off somewhat for the parade, during which the photos below were taken of the Marching Bears. However, the bottom fell out of the clouds during the game itself.

Two material acquisitions that the 1988–89 UCA Marching Bears put to good use were a whole new set of uniforms for the 136-member unit and a drill writing program to more easily facilitate creating halftime programs. Both of these purchases put smiles on the faces of Russell Langston and Steven Peterson, director and assistant director of the band, respectively. An image from the computer screen is seen above right. For the 1989–90 year the Symphonic Wind Ensemble (formerly the Concert Band) performed a series of concerts on campus and on a tour of central Arkansas locales. Marching Bear members are also shown that fall participating in the 1989 Homecoming Parade.

In the 1991 *Scroll* yearbook the following sentences accompanied photos of the school's band within its pages: "If practice is any indication of dedication and excellence, the University of Central Arkansas Marching Bear Band serves as a highly visible example with an end product that richly deserves the accolades it receives . . . The applause and reputation the band has achieved throughout the years proves that the practice and dedication is worth it." Below, drum majors Mark Wallace and Joel Johnson lead the 1991–92 UCA Band onto the field for that year's Homecoming game.

The 1992–93 Marching Bears above numbered 130 members on its roster, half of whom were music majors and, according to director Russell Langston, nearly 80 of them were on scholarship. The photo below left records the 1993–94 UCA Band in action on the field in Estes Stadium, while the picture at right shows the group supporting the football team from the stands.

The above photos of the UCA chapters of Kappa Kappa Psi and Tau Beta Sigma were featured in the 1995 *Scroll* yearbook. Both chapters have been in existence on the UCA campus and in service to the band since 1967. The 1995–96 edition of the UCA Marching Bears is shown below rehearsing in Estes Stadium and then in action during halftime of Homecoming '95. Dr. Ricky W. Brooks, with his Ph.D. from LSU, was the new Director of Bands at UCA, ably assisted on the staff by Richard Walker.

One of the special events in which the 1996–97 UCA Band was able to participate was President Clinton's reelection acceptance speech party held on the evening of November 5. After clearance by the Secret Service the group played a few marches at the celebration in Little Rock. Photos above show the band practicing and performing in Estes Stadium during football season. Below is the 1997–98 Marching Bear Band musically coaxing the team to victory and percussion members showing off new instruments intended to enhance the halftime experience.

UCA Alma Mater

From the hills and from the lowlands,
Comes the song of praise anew,
Sung by thousands of thy children.
Alma Mater, we sing to you

Then we'll unfurl our colors, the Purple and the Gray,
And in the breezes see them ever proudly sway;
They lead us upward; they lead us onward;
They lead to victory

Then let us gather 'round with loyal hearts and true,
Our Alma Mater's call obey,
Our dear old colors will live forever,
The royal Purple and the Gray.

With separate halftime shows set to the music of Gershwin and then the Beatles, the 1998–99 UCA Marching Bears entertained Estes Stadium crowds in attendance to cheer on the football team to victory. The photos above illustrate the result of arduous band rehearsals and the efforts of Dr. Ricky Brooks in getting the musicians to display their talent. Robert Kiilsgaard served as drum major for the season. Below is the photo of Tau Beta Sigma members that was printed in the 2000 *Scroll* yearbook.

UCA Fight Song

Go, Go, Fight Bears
You will lead us on to vic-to-ry!
Hey, go, go win team
Charge the field and never yield.
So Fight, Fight, Fight
We've got the spirit!
And we'll show our colors here tonight
So let's cheer the purple and gray team
Mighty Bears will win the FIGHT!

The 2000–2001 edition of the UCA Marching Bear Band is shown above posing in front of the campus Main Building with Lonnie Abbott serving as drum major. Also shown is the school's Wind Ensemble in concert during the spring semester. Pictured below is Dr. Ricky Brooks, the school's Director of Bands since 1995 and continuing in that position as this book goes to press. During the fall of 2001 Dallas Taylor and Brent Worley directed the band on the field as its drum majors.

For the 2002–03 school year the UCA Marching Bear Band marched over 160 members during halftime shows in Estes Stadium. Having adopted the tagline, "The Sound of Central Arkansas," the band was led onto the field by drum majors Marie Pokorski and John Joyner, who would serve in those positions as a team for three years. In April 2003 the UCA Wind Ensemble performed at Carnegie Hall in New York and at the Capitol in Washington, D.C. A final paragraph in the 2003 *Scroll* yearbook ended with the following sentences: "Marching band members do what they do because there is a certain thrill in combining dynamic music with stunning visuals to create an astounding display of sight and sound. Moreover, most band members choose to be a part of the group because through the time and commitment they spend, they often make more friends and more memories than the average student at UCA would ever have the chance to." The photos below are of the 2003–04 Marching Bear Band.

The 2004–05 UCA Band is shown above marching down Front Street in Conway during the 2004 Homecoming Parade and at halftime in Estes Stadium on campus. Below the 218-member 2005–06 Marching Bears were led onto the field by drum majors Marie Pokorski, Ben Dobbs and Joel Ratliff in what was UCA's final season in NCAA Divison II; they would move up to Division IAA in the fall of 2006. At the end of the 2005 season the Bears won the first two rounds in the NCAA Division II Football Championship before bowing to North Alabama in a quarterfinal game played at home in Estes Stadium before a full house with the UCA Band cheering on the team. Also shown below is the UCA Wind Ensemble in rehearsal for an on-campus concert February 6, 2006. At the time of this writing the students on campus were eagerly anticipating the university's 2007 Centennial Celebration.

Also, as this book went to press, UCA offered degrees in the area of instrumental music as follows:

- •Bachelor of Music in Performance
- •Bachelor of Music in Music Education
- •Bachelor of Arts in Music
- •Master of Music in Performance
- •Master of Music in Music Theory
- •Master of Music in Conducting
- •Master of Music in Education

Chapter Three

The Marching Musical Machine of the Mid-South

University of Arkansas at Pine Bluff
Arkansas Agricultural, Mechanical and Normal College
Arkansas Agricultural, Mechanical and Normal School
Branch Normal College

The University of Arkansas at Pine Bluff got its start as an offshoot of the U of A at Fayetteville. Originally, the UAF began as a land-grant college as a result of the Morrill Act of 1862 and the subsequent Second Morrill Act of 1866, which stipulated that a college could be established within the borders of Arkansas with the caveat that students could not be denied admission based upon race. Because of the prevailing political and racist attitudes of the time, segregation was an accepted norm in most areas of society, including education. And as a result, blacks and whites did not attend the same schools in primary, secondary, or higher educational settings. One way the board of trustees at Arkansas Industrial University (the original name of the UAF; it changed to the University of Arkansas in 1899) got around the above-mentioned Morrill Act segregation ban was by convincing the Arkansas General Assembly in 1873 to create a branch of the school in the portion of the state that would offer education to the "poorer classes," with an understanding that this meant black Arkansans without stating so in print. The town chosen as the school's location was Pine Bluff because (according to one of the school's historians, Sederick Rice) of its "booming black population" and its access to the large black population concentrated in south and east Arkansas.

At the time, ironically enough, the Arkansas superintendent of public instruction was a black man by the name of Professor Joseph Carter (J. C.) Corbin, who eventually became the first principal of the Branch Normal College, the first name so given to the institution. "Normal" was the term used at the time to refer to a school that had as its main purpose the education of students to become public school teachers—in this case, to prepare black teachers to teach black public school students. For the AIU trustees and much of the state's white population the establishment of the Branch Normal College would retain the status of educational segregation for a time, allowing for the discouragement of blacks from applying to AIU, while at the same time, furnishing higher educational opportunities for them in Pine Bluff. Professor J. C. Corbin is shown above standing in the center of the middle row with members of an informal instrumental group from Branch Normal that included some of his students in a photo dated from the school year 1888–89. Holding a Doctor of Philosophy, Corbin was known to be a lover of many types of music, was able to speak eight languages, and was very proficient in mathematics.

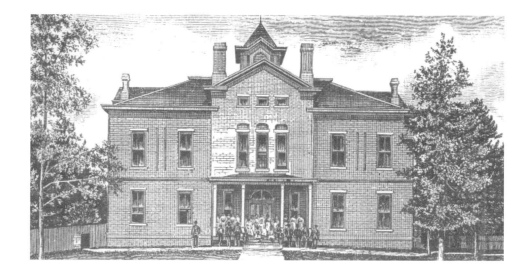

The first site of Branch Normal College was located in an existing house on the corner of Lindsay and Sevier Streets in Pine Bluff in 1875. Those streets were later renamed Second and Oak Streets, respectively. Though the house was in poor repair and school supplies were meager, Prof. Corbin opened the doors to seven students in September 1875 and saw enrollment grow to 241 by 1894. He was listed as the only instructor at the school until 1883, relying on the more advanced students to serve as student assistants. The school's first collegiate graduate was James Carter Smith, who completed his coursework in 1882. Also, in 1882, Corbin and his students moved into the first permanent brick structure built specifically for the school in western Pine Bluff near the Missouri Pacific and Southwestern railroads junction. That first brick building is shown in the illustration above.

According to the UAPB historian Sederick Rice, J. C. Corbin was also the first music teacher at the school with "various proficiencies on instruments such as the flute, piano, organ, and violin." He also placed a high emphasis on "voice practice and tone designed to augment vocal cords." A donation by a Mrs. Joseph Neely of a cabinet organ enabled students to perform music recitals and public performances. The lack of funds to purchase musical instruments made it difficult to develop much of an instrumental program at the school. Therefore, as at a number of other Arkansas schools, the vocal program preceded the success of a band or orchestra on the campus. The above photo of the auditorium of Branch Normal with the school choir on the stage of the building shown at the top of this page was taken in 1895.

J. C. Corbin remained as the principal of Branch Normal until 1902 when his contract was not renewed by the University of Arkansas Board of Trustees due to a conflict they had with his teaching philosophies. He subsequently was hired as the principal of Pine Bluff's Merrill High School, a position he held until he died in 1911. His successor at Branch Normal was Isaac S. Fisher, also a "true" lover of all kinds of music who organized one of the school's first official bands in 1902 consisting of twelve to fifteen musicians. Fisher, a graduate of Tuskegee Institute, was so determined to raise money for a decent band and organ on campus that he encouraged students to pick cotton in Arkansas fields as a fundraiser in 1907. He stated that he believed that a successful band and choir would earn good public relations for the campus and stimulate revenue for the school. In 1909 Miss Christine Rambo was hired for the new teacher of music position, relieving Fisher to concentrate on administrative duties. She remained in that role until 1917, focusing almost entirely on vocal studies while the instrumental program, according to UAPB band historian Sederick Rice and former AM&N assistant director U. G. Dalton in separate publications, maintained a band membership that "fluctuated between 25 and 50" musicians until the early 1950s. A photo documenting the school's band in 1925 is shown below right.

In 1921 Branch Normal College was renamed Arkansas Agricultural, Mechanical and Normal School (AM&N) to reflect the land-grant mission of the institution, and the campus attained standard junior college status by 1925. By 1927 as a result of Act 31 of the Arkansas Legislature, AM&N separated from the U of A campus in Fayetteville and acquired its own board of trustees. That same year the legislature approved funding for the initial phase of a new campus on the current UAPB site on North Cedar Street (now known as University Drive, part of State Highway 79). The photo above left is of Caldwell Hall, one of the first structures completed on the new site in 1929. The building was named after Senator Creed Caldwell and contained classrooms, offices, and a four-hundred-seat auditorium (see the sidebar on the final page of this chapter). In 1928 John Brown Watson became the new president of the college, and in that same year, the State Board of Education approved AM&N as a standard four-year college. Watson also wrote the alma mater for the school.

In the 1935 AM&N course catalog there is a paragraph that states: "The college sponsors a band, an orchestra, a string quartette, a chorus and a glee club. As a result music is rendered on special occasions, and from time to time musical programs are presented to the public." No photos accompany these sentences. But in the 1938 AM&N yearbook the above left photo was printed and a notation under it indicated that the band was directed by Mr. David Mells. Also mentioned: "Football games, parades, concerts and chapel exercises are graced with performances from the band." In addition, there were photos of the swing orchestra (*shown above right*) and the concert orchestra pictured in the yearbook. The photo below was taken of the AM&N Marching Band in 1940 as printed in Sederick Rice's book about the history of the school's music program entitled *Must Be the Music.* Rice also included the following sentences: "The marching band tradition continued through 1940, under the leadership of Professor Benjamin R. Durant. Durant organized pep meetings in the fall with 50-piece instrumentation for performances on the football gridiron producing school-spirited music."

When Lawrence A. Davis succeeded John Watson as president of AM&N in 1943 after Watson died suddenly in 1942, he recognized the need for a strong college band program on the campus, according to Ulysses G. Dalton III in his 1981 doctoral dissertation covering the history of the Music Department of UAPB. In an interview Davis told Dalton that an excellent band was needed for performing at athletic events, as a means for recruiting students, and as a teacher-training organization to go into public schools to teach instrumental music. And he said that he sought ways and means of securing funds to develop such a program. He signed Alma Brown as band director in 1946, who stayed for three years, and then John E. Williams, who directed the group for two more. Incidentally, Alma Brown was the first woman to hold the director position for marching and concert bands at a college or university in Arkansas.

Photos on this page are of the AM&N Orchestra that played for various social events on the campus and other locations in southeast Arkansas in 1940 (*above*) and 1947 (*below*).

As with the other college bands in Arkansas the years of World War II were bleak regarding enrollment on the AM&N campus since many male students responded to the call of military service. But after the war, college band programs rebounded, AM&N included. Though the Pine Bluff college was not funded at the level as the more predominantly white campuses in the state, the AM&N Band did find the funds to outfit the group with new uniforms as shown in the 1948 *Lion* yearbook above and the larger band from 1949 shown below. Both groups were directed by Alma L. Brown. The smaller photo below is of the college orchestra, who called themselves the "Czars of Rhythm," headed by Trenton Cooper at the piano and featuring U. G. Dalton (*third from right*), whose dissertation is cited in this text. The group was regularly heard on Tuesday nights on radio station KCLA in Pine Bluff.

The above left photo is of the 1949–50 Golden Lions Band posed on stage of the campus auditorium, while the dance band orchestra (then called the Arkansas State Collegians) sits for the photograph session above right. By Homecoming 1950, the AM&N Homecoming Parade had become a tradition in downtown Pine Bluff, drawing crowds and parade entries from not only southeast Arkansas, but neighboring states as well. Also shown below is a copy of the school's alma mater written by former AM&N president John B. Watson.

The 1952 *Lion* yearbook photo of the AM&N Marching Band above records director J. E. Williams's second and last band at the school. During the 1951–52 school year the Arkansas State Collegians (*above right*) led by George Joyner traveled quite a bit performing gigs and at one time were the leading college dance band according to the *Pittsburgh Courier* newspaper poll. In the fall of 1952 Mr. Harold Strong joined the AM&N faculty to eventually become a legend at the school. He remained as band director until the spring of 1981. In both the 1952 and 1953 *Lion* yearbooks it was mentioned that the band numbered sixty members each year, though the photos above and below from those years do not include that many musicians. Apparently not everyone showed up for picture day. Also note that Carl Reeves was listed as being drum major for the band every fall season from 1948 through 1952. The photos below reflect the membership of the 1952–53 and 1953–54 AM&N Bands, top and bottom, respectively.

Harold S. Strong
Director

Harold S. Strong graduated from the Chicago Musical College with a Master's in Music Education after having played in the 372nd Infantry Band in the army and with a jazz band in Chicago. Before going to AM&N he had also taught in the Chicago public schools. A challenge for Strong at AM&N was the recruitment of instrumental music students in the state of Arkansas. In 1952, according to Dalton in his doctoral dissertation, of the more than one hundred high schools for blacks in the state, only four had bands. And only one of those included band in the curriculum as a credit course (Dunbar High School in Little Rock). Two reasons were given: (1) a lack of funds needed to develop bands, and (2) the lack of teachers trained to organize and develop instrumental music programs. Strong's work was cut out for him. Photos on this page show the Golden Lions Marching Band for 1954–55 (*above*) and 1955–56 (*below*); also pictured is the college's stage band above for 1954–55; George Celestan served as drum major for the fall seasons from 1953 to 1955.

To expose more black high school students to the AM&N band program in the 1950s, Harold Strong scheduled the Golden Lions Marching Band to march in parades and events at places such as Memphis and the Columbia County Fair held in Magnolia each year. At times they were the only black band marching at the events and they did indeed bring in more students to the campus. In addition, some school boards with separate white and black school systems in their districts (according to Dalton's dissertation) "sought to circumvent, or at least delay, implementation of the Supreme Court's 1954 desegregation decision by upgrading the black schools." The instrumental music programs at those schools did improve with the hiring by more minority schools of graduates from AM&N. As a result, Strong's programs at the college grew in enrollment with more jobs being available. On this page are scenes of the 1956–57 AM&N Band rehearsing in their band hall on campus above and the 1957–58 band in a picture below from the *Lion* yearbook.

An example of the growth of bands in traditionally black high schools across the state of Arkansas was shown in the bands participating in the AM&N Homecoming Parade. In the early 1950s almost no Arkansas high school bands were in attendance, whereas twenty of the twenty-seven bands in the 1958 parade were directed by AM&N graduates. Above is a photo of the 1958–59 Golden Lions Band with Clarence Jones out front as drum major, and below is the 1960–61 drum major Bennie Cox with that season's majorette line and Harold Strong directing the Concert Band in a spring 1961 performance. U. G. Dalton was Strong's assistant from 1957 to 1962.

When the number of black high school bands increased in Arkansas, there was a natural progression toward competitive festivals for the musicians paralleling the existence of such in the predominantly white band community. Festivals were first held on the AM&N campus in the early 1960s, and the Arkansas State Band Directors Association for Blacks was organized to run them in 1962. Although it may appear obvious, the majority of the high school bands that participated in the festivals had directors who were alumni of AM&N. The above photos are of the 1961 Marching Lions on their home field and the Concert Band in performance in the campus auditorium. The photo below shows the 1962–63 edition of the band performing in the stands during a rainy football game at home. Assistant U. G. Dalton is shown at left directing the group.

As usual, the AM&N Golden Lions "Marching 100" was front and center during Homecoming activities in both 1964 (*above*) and 1965 (*below*) whether it was marching in the Homecoming Parade down Pine Bluff's Main Street or performing on the field during the football game. Another annual event that became a mainstay on campus was the performance of Handel's "Messiah" during the Christmas season. Choirmaster Shelton McGee directed the performance in the 1960s, and in 1965 the Little Rock Symphony Orchestra made its first appearance accompanying the AM&N Music Department's holiday presentation.

Even though the AM&N Marching Band was known as the "Marching 100" in the early 1960s, the 1966–67 group was more like the "Marching 130" as seen in the photo above. Also shown is that year's Concert Band. In 1967 the *Lion* yearbook was dedicated to Harold S. Strong, in which he was described as "Bandmaster, Maestro of the Arkansas AM&N College 'Marching 100' and the Concert Band. Dedicated, intolerant of slothful and inefficient results, perfectionist, strong in character, exacting the best from each of the young musicians to build a place for the AM&N College Band." Photos below are from the 1967–68 school year with Mr. Strong in the midst of the band in the stands during a football game and rehearsing students during a sectional class.

Above is the 1968–69 AM&N "Marching 100" in action on campus during a halftime performance from two different perspectives. Below, the photo at upper left shows the AM&N and Arkansas Tech Bands performing a joint show in War Memorial Stadium in Little Rock before the first-ever meeting of the Golden Lions and the Wonder Boys football teams in the fall of 1969. The second photo features the 1969–70 AM&N Band's majorette line strutting their stuff during that fall's Homecoming Parade in Pine Bluff. The band also was invited to perform later before a Kansas City Chiefs crowd in Kansas City when the NFL team played live over the NBC television airwaves. Notably on campus, AM&N students (band and choir members included) began using the new Isaac Hathaway Fine Arts Building during the 1969 fall semester. Hathaway was an internationally renowned African-American sculptor who lived in Pine Bluff and taught at AM&N College and Merrill Public Schools from 1915 to 1937.

The national Greek band service organizations, Kappa Kappa Psi fraternity and Tau Beta Sigma sorority, were established on the AM&N campus on November 15, 1970. The charter members are shown above for the Epsilon Chi chapter of Kappa Kappa Psi and the Delta Pi chapter of Tau Beta Sigma. Below are band director Mr. Harold Strong and his assistant during the 1970–71 school year, Tyrone Tyler, along with a portion of the band standing at attention and the band's drum major exhibiting his style.

Culminating months of often-heated discussion regarding the merger of AM&N back into the University of Arkansas System, the state's two oldest public higher educational institutions rejoined their ties on July 1, 1972, with the Pine Bluff campus renamed as the University of Arkansas at Pine Bluff.

The scenes above are from the 1972–73 marching season for the Golden Lions Band, whereas the ones below are from 1973–74. The drum major for the group was listed as Arthur "Bubble Eye" Davis during that time. When AM&N joined the University of Arkansas System in 1971, Dr. Lawrence Davis Sr. had his title changed from president of AM&N to that of chancellor of UAPB. In August 1973, Dr. Davis left the school and Johnny B. Johnson Sr. was appointed acting chancellor. On July 1, 1974, Herman B. Smith Jr. began his duties as the new chancellor.

The photos above show the two sides of the 1974–75 UAPB band program with the upper picture showing the Golden Lions Marching Band halftiming it during football season and the lower one depicting the Concert Band in performance on campus in the Hazzard Gymnasium during the Homecoming assembly in 1974. Below is the band's percussion section marking the beat during the 1974 Homecoming Parade and the majorette line that fronted the 1975–76 UAPB "Marching 100."

The 1976–77 edition of the UAPB Golden Lions Band is shown above during one of its halftime shows with a recently added flag line. The accompanying shot is of the UAPB Jazz Ensemble (begun in 1975) under the direction of its founding director and the new assistant to Harold Strong for the marching and concert bands, Odie Burrus, an alumnus of the band. Burrus would eventually succeed Strong as the school's Director of Bands. Below is Burrus (*right*) standing alongside Harold Strong and drum major William Dickerson with the 1977–78 brass section in poses for yearbook photos.

One of the highlights for 1978–79 was the appearance of the UAPB Golden Lions Band at the NFL football game between the Kansas City Chiefs and the San Diego Chargers in Kansas City in November. Above is the group marching in that year's Homecoming Parade and Homecoming halftime show. The photo below shows the 1979–80 UAPB Band posing in the campus stands with a new rifle squad joining the majorettes and flag line in front of the group during parades and halftime shows. John Wilber served as drum major for the year.

The 1980–81 school year was Harold Strong's last year as the Director of Bands at the University of Arkansas at Pine Bluff. With tenure at the school that lasted twenty-nine years, he is shown above directing the marching band from the sidelines. Odie Burrus Jr. succeeded Strong as director. The other photos show the band in lively motion marching into War Memorial Stadium and performing at home. The 130-member unit traveled to two out-of-town football games that year to Arkansas Tech and Lincoln University. Below, drum major Daniel Dykes directs the 1981–82 UAPB Marching Band during a halftime show, and the lower woodwind section poses for a yearbook photo. Dr. Herman B. Smith Jr. resigned as UAPB chancellor in June 1981, with Dr. Lloyd V. Hackley assuming that office in September.

The photos above show the 1982–83 UAPB Golden Lions Band in action on the field during a halftime show on campus led by drum major Daniel Dykes, while the shots below include Director of Bands Odie Burrus with the trumpet section and flag line as they posed for the 1984 *Lion* yearbook.

A caption in the 1986 *Lion* yearbook included the following: "Rock the Field!—under the direction of Mr. Odie Burris the band rocked football, basketball games and assemblies to UAPB's own special beat." The 1985–86 Golden Lions Band, also claiming the moniker "The Marching Musical Machine of the Mid-South," is shown above marching in the 1986 Homecoming Parade and on campus during a halftime show. The pictures below are of the 1986–87 woodwind and brass sections and the band playing in the stands. It might be worth noting that Daniel Dykes served as drum major for the Golden Lions Band each fall from 1981 through 1986, and that Dr. Charles A. Walker became the campus's new chancellor in August 1986.

After a successful kickoff of the inaugural Annual Arkansas Classic football game the previous year, the Golden Lions returned to Little Rock's War Memorial Stadium in the fall of 1988 to play the Mississippi Valley State Devils. Though the team lost the contest, the UAPB Marching Band put on a real show to delight the folks in the stands. Above the band is seen marching into the stadium as the percussion section sets the beat. In the spring of 1989 Odie E. Burrus Jr. (*below left*) retired from his position as Director of Bands at UAPB. The new maestro was Dr. Joseph Miller (*below right*), who began that fall.

For the 1990–91 school term Dr. Joseph Miller (*second from the left in the front row above*) directed the UAPB Bands with the help of three assistant directors (*from left in the front row*): Kelvin Washington, Don Parker, and Robert Elliot. The two men in the back row, Gerome Hudson (still with the band as of this writing) and Bruce McAllister, provided assistance in technical and support services. That year's 170-member band, shown spelling out the university's initials above, performed at a New Orleans Saints game in the Super Dome, a Mardi Gras Parade in New Orleans, and the Martin Luther King Parade in Florida. On an administrative note, Dr. Lawrence A. Davis Jr., the son of the school's former president and chancellor, became the campus's new chancellor in November 1991. "The Marching Musical Machine of the Mid-South" for 1991–92 is pictured below, being led during that year's Homecoming Parade by drum major Christopher Neal, along with the Concert Band performing on campus in a spring concert. Also shown are the sisters of the campus chapter's Tau Beta Sigma sorority.

In the fall of 1992 Mr. Kelvin Washington stepped up to take the director's baton of the UAPB Golden Lions Marching/Concert Band. Describing the group's musical repertoire, the yearbook stated that "it ranges from rap, rhythm and blues, oldies but goodies to classical and modern music." The band's drum majors numbered three as seen above with (*left to right*) Nina Nelson, Christopher Neal, and Chris Giles serving in those roles. The photos below feature the 1993–94 Golden Lions Marching Band backing up the Golden Girls dance team and the Concert Band performing a spring presentation under the direction of Kelvin Washington. Washington accepted the Director of Bands position at Howard University in Washington, D.C., at the end of that season.

The 1994–95 school year found the Golden Lions Marching Band with a new band director in John Graham, a Bachelor's and Master's degree graduate in Music Education from UCA in Conway. The band above shows its usual soulful style and spirit during the 1994 Homecoming Parade and, as the 1995 *Lion* yearbook captioned the other photo within its pages, "The UAPB band shows off their funky steps." Below, the 1995–96 band is shown marching in the traditional Gateway Classic Parade in St. Louis that preceded the football game against Howard University. In the battle of the bands in Busch Stadium, the "Marching Musical Machine of the Mid-South" (also referred to as "M4") brought home the trophy in the lower left photo, proudly displayed by drum majors Arthur Johnson, Ben Warner, and Mario Snelling. The group also played at the Red River Classic game against Grambling State where the Golden Lions defeated the Tigers for the first time in thirty-six years.

In the 1996 UAPB Homecoming Parade the Golden Lions Marching Band is shown in the above left photo stepping through the streets of Pine Bluff while the band's drum majors, Timothy Grant and Christopher Johnson, work their magic on the field with their batons during a halftime show. Note that Grambling came back that fall and avenged their Red River Classic loss the previous year in defeating the Golden Lions 32–15. Below is the UAPB Jazz Ensemble performing a gig on campus in the spring of 1998.

Always one of the more exciting events for the UAPB Marching Band is the trip to St. Louis in support of the football team's playing in the Gateway Classic. The fall of 1998 proved to be no exception as can be seen in the above photos. The band both performed in the parade before the game and at halftime of the game itself. Note that the band fronted no less than four drum majors that year: Ben Warner, Curtis Reed, Kevin Loring, and Christopher Johnson. The photos below are of the "Marching Musical Machine of the Mid-South" performing at the 1999 Homecoming game and the UAPB chapter of the Kappa Kappa Psi service fraternity.

For the fall of 2000 the UAPB Golden Lions Marching Band wore uniform overlays that more clearly noted the group's identity as reflected in the above photos taken during the Arkansas Classic football game played in Little Rock's War Memorial Stadium. Below, the 2001–02 Golden Girls pour on the allure as the band puts on yet another exuberant halftime show.

Director John Graham is pictured above during the 2002 football season conducting the Golden Lions Band from the sidelines, while drum majors Stephen Bailey, Rashad Hollis, Spencer Brown, and Terrence Bell led on-field drill maneuvers. The 2002–03 Golden Lions Marching Band is shown below playing in the stands of the grand Golden Lions Stadium located on the north edge of the campus. The band at the time had grown under the direction of John Graham to over 250 students including drum majors, Golden Girls (dance squad, *bottom left*), and Golden Silks (flag squad). Subsequent seasons would find the band in their own seating in stands built behind the west end zone.

The school year 2004–05 found the Golden Lions Band on the road as in years past, including a trip to St. Louis for the Gateway Classic as shown above right. That year's Golden Girls effectively present themselves to the camera in the above left photo. By 2005, the UAPB Band had grown to over 270 members including the five drum majors pictured below leading the group onto home field (the drum majors were Orin Odom, Brandon Lynch, Kelley McCuin, Phillip Stanford, and Nathaniel Williams). Notable appearances included marching at the Arkansas Classic against Alabama State and the State Farm Classic against Grambling State, both games of which were played in Pine Bluff, plus the Gateway Classic in St. Louis versus Tuskegee University. The band also performed at the Mississippi Valley State game played on Chicago's Soldier Field. The UAPB athletic program as of this writing is a proud member of the Division IAA Southwestern Athletic Conference.

The concert band program at UAPB has grown along with the marching program as far as quality and quantity of participants goes, with the bands outgrowing the physical plant provided for them years ago. As a result, the marching band rehearsed in the latter years in the Fine Arts Auditorium sitting in the audience's seats while the directors conducted from the stage. Concert band season also required that the Concert Band, which augmented the school's flagship fifty-member Wind Symphony, had to be broken into two smaller sixty-five-member Concert Bands, one designated the Black Band under the leadership of assistant director Darrell Evans and one known as the Gold Band under the guidance of assistant director Harold Fooster.

Degrees available on the UAPB campus as of this printing include the Bachelor of Science degree in Music in the following four areas:

   •Piano/Vocal Emphasis (Teaching)
   •Instrumental Emphasis (Teaching)
   •Instrumental/Piano/Vocal (Non-Teaching)
   •Sound Recording Technology

In the new UAPB Museum on the Golden Lion campus is a framed photo of a plaque that has been on the wall in Caldwell Hall since its dedication in 1929. It simply states:

> ARKANSAS STATE COLLEGE FOR NEGROES
> 1929
> ERECTED BY THE STATE OF ARKANSAS
> THE GENERAL EDUCATION BOARD AND
> THE JULIUS ROSENWALD FUND COOPERATING

Beneath the above words are listed the school's Board of Control members, the state supervisor, and the college's president, architects, and contractors. Beside the plaque's photo are the following comments about that particular name of the college:

> "Arkansas State College"
>
> During the Arkansas AM&N College era (1929–1972) the college was warmly referred to as "Arkansas State" by almost everyone associated with her. The plaque depicted here can be found in Caldwell Hall, the campus' former administration building constructed in 1929. This plaque is perhaps the primary reason that the faculty, students and alumni from around 1930 until the 1970s affectionately referred to their Alma mater as "Arkansas State College". Other reasons may include the college hymn which begins with "State College", and the college's athletic teams playing under the banner of "Arkansas State Lions". Also, the Homecoming queen was called Miss "A" State as late as 1976, even though the college's name was changed to the University of Arkansas at Pine Bluff in 1972.
>
> The original name of the institution was changed from Branch Normal College to the Arkansas Agricultural, Mechanical and Normal School in 1921, and supposedly to Arkansas AM&N College in 1927, with the separation of the school from the University of Arkansas at Fayetteville. However, the writer has found no documented evidence that the name of the institution was ever officially changed to Arkansas State College for Negroes as it appears on this building dedication plaque. This is also the first declaration of the institution as a college for Negroes.

(Author's note: The writer referred to above is the author of the comments in the museum display and not the author of this book.)

Chapter Four

The Pride of Arkansas State

Arkansas State University

Arkansas State College

State Agricultural and Mechanical
   College of Jonesboro

First District Agricultural School

Arkansas State University is one of the four current state campuses created in 1909 by the Arkansas General Assembly to provide advanced educational training needed in the predominantly agricultural economy of the nation's twenty-fifth state (see the preface for more information about the origins of these schools). Located in Jonesboro as the First District Agricultural School, this institution opened its doors to its first class in the fall of 1910 in the old downtown Elks Lodge on the corner of Main and Washington Streets. Meanwhile, the school's trustees let a contract for the first building to be constructed on its current site east of town—the original Administration Building. The site, the old Warner-Krewson estate, was next to a railroad track, which was important since many students arrived and departed from the school by train. The reader is reminded that most nonrail travel at the time involved horse-drawn vehicles driven over unpaved roads. Today, there is still an actively used set of train tracks located on the southern edge of the campus.

The first presiding officer over the First District Agricultural School in 1910 was V. C. Kays. Since the school was not yet considered a college at the time, but a specialized high school, Kays's title was that of principal. The following year the first football and basketball teams were organized on the campus and the athletes had to provide their own uniforms.

Music on the Jonesboro campus in the early days consisted of unofficial student- or faculty-led singing and self-amusement and entertainment. Occasionally, a student played along on his own guitar or other hand-held instrument to add to the merriment. In the 1911–12 catalog of the school there is mention of a beginning vocal music course offered. The 1914–15 catalog offers a general chorus class and voice and piano lessons. Also two Glee Clubs met each week and a cantata was performed during the year. An orchestra met twice a week for any students having their own wind or stringed instrument. For the next few years there was a notation in the catalog that "a brass band will also form a part of the student activities" with no further explanation.

The 1917–18 school catalog printed prior to the end of World War I stated that "every male student will be required to take [military training in the school's Military Department] and those who stay in the dormitory will be under military regulations during the entire year." Each student had to purchase his own uniform and was issued a gun for which he had to make a cash deposit.

In the early days of the war, the school's trustees were interested in establishing a Student Army Training Corps (SATC) unit on the campus, but the U.S. Army determined that such units could only be established at schools that were organized with at least a junior college curriculum. As a result the school restructured its program "to offer two-year college level training in agriculture, home economics and teaching," according to Larry Ball and William Clements in their book, *Voices from State*. Subsequently, in the early fall of 1918 the campus was granted permission to house an SATC unit, but the armistice was signed in November of that year, thus canceling the program altogether. Years later an ROTC program would find itself on the campus instead.

Although the school itself had created a two-year program in the areas listed above, the campus would not receive formal approval from the state for junior college status until the 1925 Arkansas General Assembly passed Act 45, officially granting junior college status to all four of the state's District Agricultural Schools.

The first photo this author has uncovered of an instrumental ensemble on the Jonesboro campus is the top one below of the school's orchestra found in the pages of the 1923 *Yearling* yearbook. Apparently the group was made up of college students, preparatory students from the high school in conjunction with the college's education department, faculty members, and some musicians from the community at large. No director is listed. In the second photo below of the 1923–24 orchestra, a Miss Deal is listed as that year's director. And in the third photo taken during the 1925–26 school year, Mr. R. C. Racely (*left*) is named as the group's director. The school's athletic teams were called the "Aggie Farmers" until 1925 when they were renamed the "Gorillas."

R. C. Racely (*second from left, top photo*) is once again listed as the director of the 1927–28 orchestra at State. The photo to the right above shows members of the orchestra joined by community musicians marching in a parade through Jonesboro's streets in the fall of 1927. In the fall of 1928 Racely yielded the orchestra's baton to Miss Eleanor Current (*standing to the right in the bottom photo*), who joined the faculty the previous year as the violin instructor. She held this position until the spring of 1931.

In the fall of 1929 a band appeared on the campus playing for the football game in the above photo. The *Yearling* yearbook listed the bandmaster as Guy French and the drum major as Ralph Wisner. Both were students at State. It also mentioned that State College Band's theme song was "Piccolo Pete." Note that the banner in the above photo states "A & M Band"; it should be remembered that the four District Agricultural Schools were renamed as Agricultural and Mechanical Junior Colleges by the Arkansas General Assembly in 1925, save for the Second District School, which was renamed Arkansas Polytechnic Junior College. The school's mascot changed again in 1930 from the "Gorillas" to the "Indians." Also, authorization was granted for the establishment of a four-year college curriculum on the State campus in 1930. During the 1930–31 school year French and Wisner were still in their leadership positions, but the group had grown to twenty-three listed musicians clad in the caped uniforms pictured below. The State orchestra (*also shown below*) directed by Eleanor Current (*at right with baton*) played live concerts over the radio during the year of extension work performances they gave in Memphis, Little Rock, and Hot Springs.

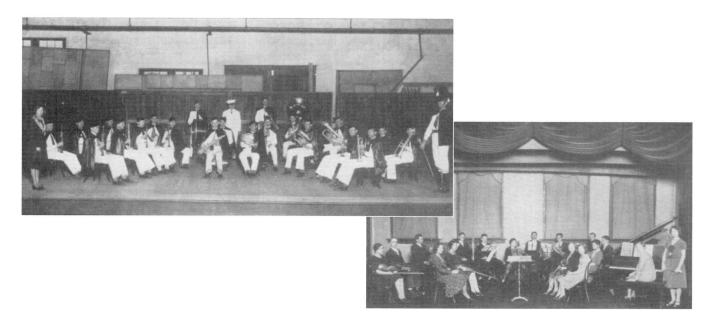

The State Band for 1931–32 shown above changed its look from the year before by the wearing of dark pants instead of white pants under the black capes lined in red. Guy French, who had directed the band for the three years he was an undergraduate, graduated in 1932 and stayed on as a faculty member at State through the first year that the band merged with the ROTC program in 1936. French also directed the campus orchestra until 1937. Below are the Arkansas State College Band and the Arkansas State College Orchestra for 1932–33. Although photos from both school years represented on this page show the name "Arkansas State" on the bass drum head, the Arkansas General Assembly did not officially change the name of the school as such until it passed Act 222 in 1933.

Even in the midst of the economic Depression of the 1930s there was a band on the Arkansas State campus. The 1933–34 ASC Band is pictured above. In 1936 when there was the establishment of a ROTC unit at the school the band program merged into it benefiting with uniforms and the purchase of some much-needed instruments. Seen below are the 1936–37 campus orchestra and ROTC Band both directed by the newly commissioned Lieutenant Guy French. Also on campus was the very popular Collegians Dance Orchestra directed by Lewis Davis. The Collegians was actually begun by Guy French during his undergraduate days at A-State, though at the time it was spelled "Kollegians."

Guy French

Lewis Davis

For the 1937–38 school year with French no longer at the school, Arkansas State hired Mrs. Earl Hazel as the orchestra's conductor and the ROTC Band was led by a student, Captain John Horn. The State Collegians Dance Orchestra was directed by student musician Lloyd Hancock, seen playing sax in the middle of the front row above. The following year both the State Collegians and the ROTC Band (*below*) were directed by Hancock.

Lloyd Hancock

In 1939 Lester Somers (*top right*) was hired as the new director of the Arkansas State Orchestra and led the group in presenting concerts at a number of high schools in northeast Arkansas as well as presenting its own concerts on campus, accompanying the Jonesboro Choral Club in presenting the *Messiah* and joining the Jonesboro Symphonic Orchestra on occasion in concert. He also oversaw the ROTC Band for the 1939–40 school year shown above and 1940–41 shown below. The dance orchestra changed its name to "The Statesmen" for 1940–41 and was directed that year by Charles Moyers (*bottom inset*).

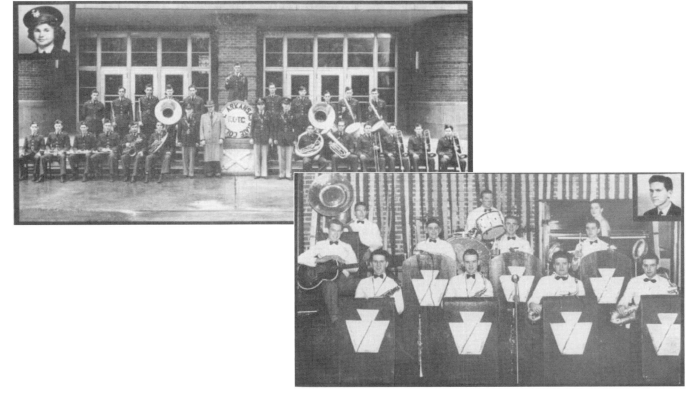

According to the school historian Lee A. Dew in his book *The ASU Story*, the A-State campus took a big hit in enrollment at the beginning of 1941. He wrote, "World War II meant the end of all effective fine arts programs for the duration. The small civilian enrollment did not enroll in such courses. The faculty was reduced and the physical facilities largely turned over to the army." Intercollegiate athletics were also temporarily disbanded. ASC was used at various times to train units of the Army Administration School, Army Air Cadets, and an Army Specialized Program in engineering.

The ROTC program at ASC was also put on hold due to the war, thereby removing a band program from the campus. Without ROTC and football and basketball teams to support, an organized band at Arkansas State was deemed unnecessary at the time.

Again referencing Dr. Dew's book, "The first post-war band was organized in 1946 by professor James L. Patty and made its debut at Homecoming that year, where it presented a chapel program in the morning, played at the football game in the afternoon, and provided music for the Homecoming dance at night. Robert Leet was drum major, assisted by four majorettes. The band had twenty-six musicians." The photos below of the band are from the 1947 *Indian* yearbook (the name of the yearbook was changed from the *Yearling* in 1937). Performing on the campus that year was "The Southernaires Orchestra."

Above can be seen the 1947–48 ASC Band under the direction of James L. Patty (*top left*) and the campus dance band. The *Indian* yearbook indicated that the band went on a northeast Arkansas tour of high schools that spring and that the highlight of the fall term had been marching in the Memphis Cotton Carnival Parade. The photo below left is of the 1948–49 ASC Band led by drum major George Lyle posed on stage of the Commons Building, later named State Hall and most recently the College of Nursing and Health Professions.

Once more quoting Lee Dew: "The college orchestra was revived in 1949, with fourteen members, and vocal music was also well under way again. By 1950 the orchestra reached its postwar peak of twenty-one members, and began to decline. By 1955 the 'orchestra' was only a dance band, with no stringed instruments, and the following year the name 'orchestra' was dropped." The photo below right is of the "revived" orchestra in 1949.

The 1949–50 ASC Marching Band is shown above in what would become their traditional formation of the "A" used for the playing of the alma mater at football games. Eddie Groblebe served that year in his first of four seasons as the band's drum major. Below are the ASC Band and majorette line for 1950–51 with the band's new director Kenneth G. Appleton shown standing in the back row right.

The photos above show the ASC Arts Building, which housed the band's rehearsal hall, practice rooms, and storage area in the 1950s and 1960s. The room where the band is shown practicing above is located on the first floor to the right in the Arts Building photo. In February 1952 the ASC Band marched in the New Orleans Mardi Gras Parade. According to Lee Dew, "Forty-five members made the trip, the cost of which was paid for by a fund contributed by faculty members and townspeople of Jonesboro." The photos below are of the 1952–53 ASC Band and its majorette line.

The 1953–54 Arkansas State Band is shown above with director Kenneth Appleton standing in the doorway of the bus. The Great Southern Coaches bus line was frequent transport for the band, including a trip to the Tangerine Bowl (*left*) that year against East Texas. The game ended in a 7–7 tie. Donald R. Minx, who would become a legend at ASC, signed on as Director of Bands at the school in the fall of 1954. He is shown below directing the band during a campus pep rally with the twirlers helping to stir up team spirit. Also below is the school's stage band for 1954–55.

Donald R. Minx
Assistant Professor of Music
and Director of Bands

Orchestra

The 1955–56 ASC Band is shown above in concert formation in front of the Administration Building on campus, while that year's Dance Band is positioned in the school's ballroom. The bands' director is seated second from left in the front row of the Dance Band holding a tenor saxophone. Below, the 1956–57 ASC Band accompanied the football team to Little Rock for that season's NAIA Aluminum Bowl played in War Memorial Stadium in the rain. A photo of both bands participating in the combined half-time show appears on page 181 in the Arkansas Tech chapter of this book. Drum major Jimmy Stimson and the 1956–57 majorette line are also shown below.

The longer Don R. Minx remained at Arkansas State as the Director of Bands, the better the reputation its bands received. By 1956 about half the band students were on some type of grant-in-aid program assisting with tuition costs. The 1957–58 ASU Band shown above marched at a number of high school marching exhibitions and the Concert Band went on a Mid-South tour in the spring appearing at various high schools. Norman Todenhoft was Minx's assistant director and Danny Bosche (*above*) was drum major for the 1957–58 band. A familiar sound at ASC football games for 1958–59 was "Good afternoon, football fans, this is your halftime announcer for the Marching Indian Band." Outfitted in uniforms of scarlet, gold, and black and led by drum major Larry Maness, the band is shown below performing a halftime show on the A-State home field. Also shown is the A-State pep band playing at a home basketball game.

The 1959–60 A-State Marching Band is shown above in the stands on campus supporting the Indians in another contest on the gridiron while that year's enlarged Concert Band appears in the gym for a sitting with the yearbook photographer. Under director Donald Minx the 1960–61 Arkansas State Marching Indians became known as "The Pride of Arkansas State," and Minx was honored at the Southeast Missouri Band Festival with the mass band formation pictured below where the Marching Indians were the featured band. They also earned an invitation to march in President John Kennedy's Inaugural Parade in January 1961. Larry Maness served as the school's drum major for his final year that season.

Don R. Minx was receiving so many accolades for the performances of the Arkansas State Band at halftime shows, parades, and concerts that the college declared November 11, 1961, as "Don Minx Day," celebrated by a special halftime show during the A-State vs. Wisconsin State game. The photos above are from the 1961–62 marching season showing the band at rehearsal on the field and that year's twirling delegation, who served along with drum major Neal Peevey. The 1962–63 edition of the Marching Indians is shown below spelling out the school's monogram and the very popular "Bill Bell and the Tribe" Dance Band is snapped in performance. Bell was a student in the A-State Band program. Minx's assistants for the year were Harold Worman and Jan Seifert.

The ninety-three-member Marching Indians for 1963–64 are shown above along with a photo of the percussion section during a field rehearsal that year. Drum major John Erwin, standing in the middle of the top row of the group photo, served as the group's drum major from 1962 to 1966. During the 1964–65 school year, in addition to all the regular Indian football games, parades, concerts, and community events, the Marching Indians were also invited to perform live at halftime for a St. Louis Cardinal NFL game (*shown below*). John Alexander, an excellent classical and jazz trumpet player, joined the band's staff as assistant director that season.

In addition to being invited back for a second time during the 1965–66 school year to Busch Stadium to perform during a St. Louis Cardinal halftime show, the ASC band also added to the campus local chapters of Kappa Kappa Psi and Tau Beta Sigma, the national band service fraternity and sorority. Charter members of those groups are shown above. The big news for the 1966–67 year was that Governor Winthrop Rockefeller signed a bill on January 17 changing ASC to university status with the school's name becoming Arkansas State University effective July 1, 1967. The band's calendar for the 1966–67 season included marching in the Arkansas Livestock Exposition Parade in Little Rock and the Jonesboro Christmas Parade, performing for the out-of-town Murray State football game, and presenting a concert at the Mid-South Fair. The photo below shows the 120-member band in action that fall. The young man in white lunging on the near sidelines is feature twirler Ben Coonfield.

Drum major Ross Beck led the 1967–68 Marching Indians through a season that saw the band performing halftime shows in the on-campus Kays Stadium and in War Memorial Stadium in Little Rock. The 126 musicians who performed in the group are shown above performing a concert in the campus gym. The Concert Band for 1968–69 below is shown in their new rehearsal hall along with a photo of that year's Tribe Dance Band.

As in 1968 the A-State Indians ended the next football season as Southland Conference Champions and earned a return visit to the Pecan Bowl in Arlington, Texas. But unlike the previous year, the team came home a winner in the 1969 bowl game with a victory over Drake University, 29–21. The band and majorettes for ASU in 1969–70 are pictured above. The 1970–71 football and basketball seasons were even better for A-State in that the football team went 11–0 for the first undefeated/untied season in the history of the school, and the basketball Indians won their conference championship. The teams also made history by becoming the first Southland Conference school to win both the football and basketball championships in the same school year. Photos from the band's 1970–71 season led by drum major Doug Moore are shown below. Note the new flag squad.

Two familiar sights and sounds on the 1971–72 A-State campus were The Tribe stage band above left and the Director of Bands Don Minx yelling instructions through his bull horn to Marching Indians led by drum major Doug Moore during halftime rehearsals. In 1972–73 the Arkansas State Band got a lot of experience putting their halftime rehearsals to good effect by marching shows both in Little Rock's War Memorial Stadium (*below left*) and in the on-campus Kays Stadium (*below right*). The occasion of the Little Rock appearance saw the Indians competing against number-one Louisiana Tech in the hopes of an upset. It didn't happen.

At the end of the 1973 fall football season Kays Stadium on campus was closed with an ASU win over UT–Arlington 30–14. It capped thirty-six seasons of football played in that venue. The ASU Band photos above are from the 1973–74 season. For the 1974–75 season the ASU Indians football team played in a new stadium on campus, while in women's athletics, Lady Indians basketball began NCAA competition. Below the ASU Marching Indians spell out "U – S – A" on the field of the new stadium and stand in the end zone prior to halftime of the Northeast Louisiana game. It was Homecoming and A-State won 17–14. Randy Erwin was the ASU drum major for four years beginning with the fall of 1972.

One of the most common themes for football halftime shows in the fall of 1975 was the USA's celebration of its Bicentennial; it was no different at ASU. The "1–7–7–6" formation above on the ASU field was also followed by an outline of the map of the United States. Director Donald R. Minx was also a big believer in "Band Days" where secondary school bands were invited as guests to appear on the field at halftime and play with the ASU Band. So many bands came that the field was literally covered with musicians and Minx had to conduct the music from a boom bucket as seen above. Also shown above is drum major Randy Erwin among the 1975–76 ASU majorettes. Most important for the football team, the school moved up from Division II status to Division I competition in the fall of 1975. Below the 1976–77 Marching Indians under the field direction of drum major Jim Helman are shown performing at the half of the Southern Illinois game played in Little Rock's War Memorial Stadium.

For the 1977–78 school year the Marching Indians obtained new uniforms that sported the trendy bolero-styled tops and waist sashes as shown above. The other photo is of the ASU Trombone Choir directed by Neale Bartee (*seated on the steps with the baton*). An example of Director Minx's gargantuan appetite for mass bands during Band Day festivities in the fall of 1978 is the display below of 3,000 area junior and senior high band students joining the ASU Band in spelling out "M-A-R-I-A." The theme for the show was music from *West Side Story*. Minx is positioned in the boom bucket on the back of the truck on the near sidelines. The other photo is a ground-level shot of the Indian percussion section.

As in every other year the ASU Band program supported both the football and basketball teams on campus during 1979–80. The Pep Band above left is shown playing for a game in the field house, while the majorettes practice their smiles for the camera. Jimmy McCarty (*at right*) was drum major for the season. Members of the 1980–81 Marching Indians are shown below sounding out their best in support of the team and the university.

Donald R. Minx
Chairman, Department of Music

In the fall of the 1981–82 school year, the Marching Indians led on the field by drum majors Sherry Turnbow and Tommy Duffel executed their usual excellent halftime shows and made their director proud as always. But early in 1982 the Director of Bands Donald R. Minx had a heart attack and died, leaving a legacy of excellence in performance and almost thirty years of well-trained musicians to join his family and colleagues in mourning his passing. Also shown above is the 1981–82 ASU Concert Band tuba-euphonium section. Tom O'Connor stepped in to direct the ASU Bands after Minx died and led the organization from 1982 to 1988. Below the 1982–83 A-State Band is shown on the field of Injun Joe during a halftime show with the saxophone section front and center.

Another example of the large number of junior and senior high school band musicians that showed up for ASU's annual Band Day is the one above pictured from the fall of 1983. Note the row upon row of flags surrounding the perimeter of the word "M-U-S-I-C." Also above are the 1983–84 ASU majorettes. The photos below are of the 1984–85 Marching Indians in performance on the field and in the stands. Chris Hopper (*below right*) served as drum major for four seasons, 1982–85.

For the 1985–86 marching season the ASU Band acquired the above new uniforms, which had a tuxedo flair. Also shown is the band during concert season rehearsing in the band hall on campus. Below is part of the 1986–87 ASU Brass Section setting the stage for yet another spectacular Homecoming show and the majorette line, which twirled during games as drum majors Anna Talbot and Jose Feliciano (*left*) directed the shows. Talbot and Feliciano served together as a team for three years.

The two photos above from the 1987–88 school year show how the ASU Band gets involved in the action at both football (*left*) and basketball games. Below the new ASU Band director in the fall of 1988, Pat Brumbaugh, uses the familiar bullhorn to get her point across during marching rehearsal. Brumbaugh, to date, is only one of three women who have directed both a marching and concert band program on a college campus in Arkansas. Also shown below is the ASU Alumni Band playing in the stands during Homecoming 1988.

The scenes above and left are of the 1989–90 Marching Indians performing in their home stadium while the photo to the right is of Shane Fudge playing the Indian Fight Song at a basketball game in the field house. Below, members of the 1990–91 A-State Band are shown on the field in halftime performance and during a pep rally getting ready for a game. David Sanderson and Joey Fisher served as drum majors for both seasons represented on this page.

For the 1991–92 school year the Marching Indians performed in new uniforms received the previous year, but the unusually warm season saw the band often wearing the above T-shirts during halftime performances. The majorettes' attire suited them perfectly. The black and red uniforms trimmed in white can be seen on the 1992–93 A-State Band members below. On campus for that school year also was a new band director in Tom O'Neal with Michael Beard, Brandon Robinson (pictured), and Leigh Ledbetter serving as the band's drum majors. Below is the ASU Pep Band, newly renamed the "War Party," playing in the new Convocation Center, home of Indian basketball, which opened the previous year. The directors of the "War Party" were ASU alum Milton Harbison and graduate assistant Greg Bruner.

The 1993–94 edition of the Marching Indians boasted 100 members not counting the majorettes and flag line. The above photo shows the band performing at halftime with the theme of "Summertime" at the Northeast Louisiana game. Also shown is the ASU Wind Ensemble conducted by Dr. Tom O'Neal rehearsing in the band hall on campus. Members of the 1994–95 ASU Marching Indians leave the field below after a pregame performance, while flag line members parade across the field at halftime. The entire band numbered 141 in enrollment, directed on the field by Brandon Robinson, Leigh Ledbetter, and Steve Vaughn. New to the band staff was assistant director Ed Alexander.

Members of the sousaphone section of the 1995–96 Marching Indians above practice their positioning on the field for a halftime show that season. And in the photo to the right the band shows the results of all that rehearsal with a polished presentation. Below the 1996–97 A-State Band, under the direction of Dr. Thomas O'Neal and commanded on the field by drum majors Steven Vaughn, Mark Clem, and Jennifer Stone, demonstrates school spirit with musical performances on the football field and also in the Convocation Center basketball arena.

One of the popular football halftime show themes of 1997–98 was *Star Wars* music, capitalizing on the release of the first film in the second trilogy in that series. The ASU Band joined in that craze that swept America's youth and put on a presentation showcasing the band's strengths. Beginning that season Ed Alexander ascended to the director's position of the ASU Marching Band. The photos above were taken during rehearsal and showtime in 1997–98. Below, the 1998–99 A-State Band marched 142 musicians during football season with three drum majors, Jennifer Stone, Derrick Fox, and Emily Heern. Also shown below are members of the "War Party" basketball pep band supporting the team in the Convocation Center.

The 1999–2000 Marching Indians were led on the field by drum majors Derrick Fox, Emily Heern, and David Robinson and featured the majorette line shown above. Besides the usual performance for pep rallies, halftime shows, area marching competitions, and tailgate parties prior to home football games, the A-State Band played for the annual Order of the Tribe. Ed Alexander was director of the Marching Indians and the Tribe Stage Band and served as the assistant Director of Bands, while Dr. Thomas O'Neal directed the Symphonic Band and held the position of Director of Bands. The photos below are from the 2000–2001 school year. The majorette line for the latter year won the title of Arkansas State Champions in the college division at the National Baton Twirling Association Competition, vying against other college-level lines from across the state.

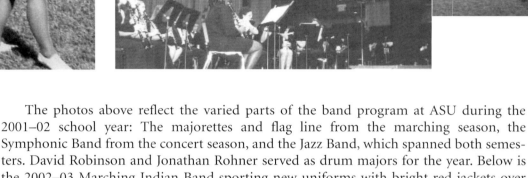

The photos above reflect the varied parts of the band program at ASU during the 2001–02 school year: The majorettes and flag line from the marching season, the Symphonic Band from the concert season, and the Jazz Band, which spanned both semesters. David Robinson and Jonathan Rohner served as drum majors for the year. Below is the 2002–03 Marching Indian Band sporting new uniforms with bright red jackets over black trousers. They are shown during a halftime performance against San Jose State in War Memorial Stadium in Little Rock. That season Director of Bands Ed Alexander welcomed Kenneth Carroll to the staff as assistant Director of Bands. Robinson (*pictured below*) and Rohner were joined by Forrest Rodgers as drum majors for the season.

The photos above show the Marching Indian and Symphonic Band components of the ASU Band program on the Jonesboro campus as were represented for the 2003–04 school year. Jonathan Rohner, Forrest Rodgers, and Ashley McBryde served as field drum majors that season. And below are pictured the 2004–05 saxophone section in sideline action, the drumline in pep rally mode, and the concert brass in performance.

During the fall of 2005 the ASU Indians football team, competing in the Division IA Sun Belt Conference, won the right to play in a bowl game for the first time in years, appearing in the New Orleans Bowl held in Lafayette, Louisiana, due to the relocation of the venue as a result of destruction caused by Hurricanes Katrina and Rita the previous August. Southern Mississippi won the game 31–6. Drum majors for the 150-member ASU Band were Ashley McBryde, Kate Puckett, and Jeremy Wortham. The photos above are from Homecoming 2005 celebrated in Indian Stadium. In the spring of 2006 Ed Alexander announced his retirement from his position of Director of Bands at ASU, and Kenneth Carroll assumed the position of Interim Director until the school's search committee decided on Alexander's successor.

As this book went to press ASU students in instrumental music could take advantage of the following degree offerings:

- Bachelor of Arts in Music
- Bachelor of Music in Instrumental Performance
- Bachelor of Music Education in Instrumental Music
- Master of Music in Instrumental Performance
- Master of Music Education

Arkansas State University Alma Mater

Our Alma Mater A.S.U.
Your hallowed halls shall ring
With praise by daughter
And noble son
Who proudly stand and sing
Mem'ries of your stirring glory
And of youthful friends we knew
The red and black
Shall ever wave
On high for A.S.U.

Chapter Five

Band of Distinction

Arkansas Tech University
Arkansas Polytechnic College
Second District Agricultural School

When the campus known today as Arkansas Tech actually opened to student enrollment in the fall of 1910 after having been created the previous year by an act of the Arkansas General Assembly, it was known as the Second District Agricultural School (see the preface for details regarding the four District Agricultural Schools). It was also primarily a specialized high school, which had as its very first student to enroll the man who would later become the school's first band director. He was Marvin Williamson, who lived on land next to that of the school and who left the school after just one year of study. Later, as he recalled in an interview in 1959 printed in the *Arkansas Gazette*, he was drafted in 1913 to direct the first band organized by the school. Williamson is shown with his first band standing to the extreme right in the above photo from the school's 1913 *Agricola* yearbook. Although eleven members are shown in the photo, fifteen were listed on the facing page of the yearbook.

Marvin Williamson's second band is shown above with the director fourth from the left in the back row in this 1914 photo. Though Williamson was in charge of both the orchestra and band programs, he had no academic credentials other than his one year spent at the Second District Agricultural School in 1910–11. His natural leadership skill and artistic talent got him through. This must have been enough because he remained on the faculty of the school until his retirement in 1956.

The above photo from the 1914 *Agricola* shows Williamson standing at right with the school orchestra. The band and orchestra had a number of men who played in both groups, though at the time only men played in the band. The women pictured were piano and stringed instrument students from the Music Department.

According to the 1915 *Agricola* yearbook, the band at the Second District Agricultural School had grown both in size and quality since its inception in 1912. Sixteen members were listed in the yearbook, including director Williamson, and the following sentences were mentioned: "The instruments are furnished by the school, thus giving many talented students a chance to broaden their musical education. The frequent concerts given by the band are greatly appreciated by all."

The two photos on this page reflect the membership of the bands at the Second District Agricultural School as recorded in the 1916 (*top*) and 1917 (*bottom*) *Agricola* yearbooks. Since football was begun at the school in 1911 and played continuously on the intercollegiate level until World War II (save for the 1918 season), it is presumed that the band played on the sidelines to increase the "pep" at ballgames during these early years.

Director Marvin Williamson stands to the extreme right front in the 1916 photo and to the extreme left front in the one from 1917.

The top photo is the 1917–18 band as pictured in the 1918 *Agricola*. The yearbook was not published again until the 1922 edition, so no photos from that publication exist of the band during the interim. The bottom left photo on this page is of the band from the 1921–22 school year and the one at bottom right is of the 1922–23 band. Note that in all of the pictures of the band from 1912 to 1922 all of the members were male. In the 1922–23 photo below a woman appears for the first time with the group—she was a saxophone player by the name of Edna Hood.

As for the school in general, it continued to be an agricultural high school until 1921 when college classes were added to the curriculum. And in 1925 the Arkansas General Assembly officially changed the school's name with Act 45 to Arkansas Polytechnic College, a junior college with the ability to grant degrees. As reported in an article in the *Arkansas Democrat Magazine* in July 1954 by Bill Hamilton, "the four years of preparatory school were dropped, one at a time, the last high school being the class of 1929." And as for intercollegiate basketball, save for an unsuccessful attempt to introduce the sport on the campus in 1914, roundball became a permanent fixture on the campus beginning with the 1922–23 season.

The top photo showcases the 1923–24 Second District Agricultural School Band with yet another woman being added to the group. Miss Hood was joined by sister saxophonist, Miss Sylvia Hurley.

For 1924–25 the bass drum in the foreground was clearly marked as establishing the locale of the band and that students were primarily agriculture students—or Aggies for short. In fact, at the time all four District Agricultural Schools' students were known as Aggies. But in the *Agricola* yearbook of 1925 a short sentence about the band introduced a new athletic nickname into the school's lexicon: "The band lends amusement to the student body by furnishing interesting programs on different occasions and the members of the band deserve part of the honor for every victory won by the 'Wonder Boys' on the gridiron, diamond, court or track." Marvin Williamson was still listed as the director of both the orchestra and the band.

BAND

ORCHESTRA

The above two photos from the 1926 *Agricola* show both the band and the orchestra at Arkansas Tech, the main difference in personnel being a few more women added to the orchestra who played stringed instruments. Also note that both organizations were wearing uniforms for the first time. The photo of the 1926–27 band at the bottom of the page shows the group wearing the same uniforms but without the white overwraps on the caps.

Marvin Williamson is shown in the above photo fronting the 1927–28 Arkansas Tech orchestra (no photo of the band appeared in that year's *Agricola*). In the 1929 *Agricola* in an article about the school's music department were these two paragraphs:

"Marvin Williamson, director of the orchestra, has given Tech much publicity by his programs on different occasions and over radio. He is the only instructor that has been with the college since its beginning and has grown with the college. He became nationally known several years ago when he directed the band on the 'Arkansas On Wheels' excursion through the Atlantic seaboard and eastern states, and on the West Point special in 1924 through the East, Middle West, and Canada.

"This year the department has carried out a great program. On the first Friday of each month the orchestra has broadcast a one-hour program from KLRA, Columbia Chain station, at Little Rock. This program has been varied by numbers from the Glee Clubs and Quartettes. During the year the music students have aided the churches and organizations of Russellville by special programs."

By the 1929–30 school year at Tech a number of changes had occurred in the campus athletic program and with the band. Two years previous the Tech basketball team had started playing as members of the Arkansas Intercollegiate Conference, while the football team only began competing in the conference in the fall of 1929. Note in the above photo of the band that a very popular women's drum corps and mascot had been added to the group playing at football games and other events. Mr. Williamson also modified his uniform attire with a white plumed hat and baton as seen at right.

By the 1931–32 school year the Arkansas Tech Band was a well-traveled organization, attending every out-of-town football game, marching in the Armistice Day Parade in Little Rock, and playing at the state track meet in Conway, a father-son banquet in Ola, and a George Washington birthday party at Altus. During the year, Director Williamson was in charge of the dance orchestra (*pictured at top*), the women's drum corps (*center*), the band (*bottom photo*), and the orchestra (*not pictured*). The dance orchestra came into existence as a direct result of the dropping of a ban that had been in effect on campus against dances at the time. Also it should be mentioned that the Wonder Boys won the 1931 AIC Football Championship with a 5–0–2 record.

For 1932–33 the Tech Band expanded the longer bugle element to the Drum Corps, which can be seen in the center of the above photo. During the school year the dance orchestra was dubbed "George and His Golden Greens," which took its name after Williamson's nickname (George) and the campus's adopted school colors. The photos below are of the Tech Band and "George and His Golden Greens" from the 1934 *Agricola*.

By the mid-1930s recovery from the impact of the Depression was slow in coming and the concert orchestra aspect of the Tech Music Department disappeared for a while. But as can be seen in the above photos from the 1935 Agricola the band was still at full strength, shown marching on campus in the photo at left and on the sidelines of a football game in the photo at right. Leonard (Skeets) Morris was drum major for the 1934 and 1935 bands. It should be inserted here that the band was in complete support of the football team in 1935 when the Wonder Boys won their second AIC Championship that fall. In a 1936 photo below, the "George and His Golden Greens" dance orchestra is posed for the camera in the school's gymnasium/auditorium.

As a political and military storm was fomenting on the European continent, life in the States was trying to get back to a level of normalcy regarding the economy and society. Franklin Roosevelt's programs were beginning to help, and colleges and universities were beneficiaries of some of those programs, in particular, new buildings on campuses. Arkansas Tech was one of those colleges. The photo above is of the Tech Band in the 1937 *Agricola* with James Francis serving as drum major (*holding the baton*). The following year Mary Croom (*in right photo*) was the twirling drum major. And in 1938–39 two drum majors fronted the band at games and parades. They were James Paul Howard and Marion Linton, seen standing at extreme left in the photo below.

At the turn of the decade the Tech Band assembled for a yearbook photo (*at top*) without about ten members according to a listing in the 1940 *Agricola*. Al Gene Jordan was named as student director, and Hales Linvall was that season's drum major. The left photo above shows the Dance Orchestra (no longer referred to in the yearbooks as "George and His Golden Greens") playing for a campus activity, and the right photo records the band playing in the stands at a 1939 football game. Also take note that in 1939 the Wonder Boys won the AIC Football Championship for the third time in eleven years with a 7–0–2 record. The bottom photo shows drum major Elizabeth Martin strutting her stuff as the 1940 Arkansas Tech Band takes to the field.

Director Williamson took on an assistant director for the school year 1941–42. He was C. A. Hartley (*shown in the first row, extreme right of the upper photo*). Hartley also took on the responsibility as director of the Dance Orchestra, but the group disbanded shortly after the beginning of the second semester; large numbers of men had left both the school and the band as a result of the bombing of Pearl Harbor on December 7 and America's entry into war against Japan. During the fall of 1941 John Haney served the band as its drum major (he is standing in the second row, extreme right). The bottom photo shows the Hartley-led Dance Orchestra in action during the first semester. Hartley did not return for the next school year.

As with the rest of American life World War II took its toll on activities on the Arkansas Tech campus. In fact, as with many other colleges, the calendar was altered from the semester schedule to quarter terms to enable the school to be used for army and navy preflight training courses in conjunction with the nearby airstrip. Male students left the regular curriculum in droves to join the military, leaving the civilian classes primarily populated with women. The Tech Band was obviously smaller in 1942–43 and over half of its membership was female as can be seen in the above photo. Particularly hard hit were the school's athletic teams, which abandoned intercollegiate play from September 1942 until January 1944. Yearbooks were not printed for the years 1943–44 and 1944–45.

After the end of World War II there was a huge increase in male enrollment in America's colleges and universities due to the GI Bill, and Arkansas Tech was no exception. Tech's band also saw a rise in numbers and a return of more men into its ranks. The 1946 *Agricola* photo above shows a modest increase in the size of the band, but the following years would see more dramatic enrollment numbers.

The above photo shows the Arkansas Tech Band in a concert setting arrangement from 1946–47, while the photos below display the band in an outdoor pose in front of the Main Building with drum major Hal Wyrick and entertaining the fans at a Wonder Boys football game in 1947–48.

In 1948 the board of trustees at Arkansas Tech voted to increase its course offerings from that of a junior college to that of a four-year institution granting degrees with the first baccalaureate diplomas awarded at the end of the 1949–50 spring semester. Other good news on the campus was that when intercollegiate sports were reintroduced after World War II ended, the football team went on a five-year streak of winning the AIC Championship from 1945 through 1949, while the basketball team won the AIC honors for seven consecutive seasons from 1949–50 through 1954–55. Those were all the more reasons for the Tech Band to show its support for the Wonder Boys as seen in the above photo from 1948–49 (note the five new majorettes behind the drum major) and in the Homecoming Parade photo below from 1949–50. Also shown below is the Dance Orchestra under the direction of drummer Ed Chesnutt.

Marvin M. Williamson

Gene Witherspoon
Director

The fall of 1950 marked a dramatic change in the history of the Arkansas Tech Band. Marvin Williamson, who had been director of the group since its inception in 1912, stepped down from the podium and handed over the baton to a man who would become another institution on the campus, Gene Witherspoon, a graduate from the University of Arkansas at Fayetteville. Though Williamson gave up the band's directorship, he remained on the music faculty until retirement in 1956. The above group photo is of the 1949–50 Tech Band with Witherspoon at the apex of the formation with his drum major Bobby Jim Needham and twirler Betty Thompson.

Under Witherspoon all the instrumental music groups on campus grew in size and quality of performance. In 1951–52 the Dance Orchestra played for an increasingly large number of engagements on and off campus (including campus radio station KXRJ), while the Concert Band displayed their own aptitude for outstanding music literature along with some popular lighter fare. Both groups are shown in the above photos from that school year.

A noticeable improvement for the Arkansas Tech Band was the acquisition of new uniforms for the fall 1952 season as can be seen above. Out in front is Eddie Epperson (who would later become the band director of SAU) in his second of four seasons as drum major, followed by feature twirler Le Roy Dickinson. The Concert Band of 1952–53 is also shown above. Homer Brown, later the renowned director of the ASTC (and then SCA) Band in Conway, was assistant director and woodwind instructor at Tech as well as the director of the Dance Orchestra.

In the early years of Witherspoon's tenure as Director of Bands at Arkansas Tech, the ROTC Band was also under his leadership. As the years progressed, directing the group became the responsibility of student cadets, with Witherspoon remaining in an advisory role. The photo below shows the ROTC Band practicing parade drills with a company of cadets following in this photo from the 1953 *Agricola*.

The Tech Band is shown above marching up Russellville's Main Street during the 1953 Homecoming Parade. The Dance Orchestra became so popular that Witherspoon created two such groups to satisfy the demand for engagements on and off campus including radio and television broadcasts. The photo below from 1954 presents the group with its new name: the Esquires. The other photo below is of the basketball Pep Band directed by Witherspoon at a game in the spring of 1955. Regarding the football team, the Wonder Boys won the AIC Championship in 1954 with a 6–1 record in conference and 8–1 overall. The men's basketball team, in addition to winning the AIC Championship seven years in a row as previously mentioned, also made seven appearances in the NAIA Tournament including twice getting to the Final Four in 1954 and 1955.

One of the innovations that Gene "Chief" Witherspoon introduced into the Arkansas Tech Concert Band's schedule was a series of Sunday concerts, which was commented upon in the 1956 *Agricola* as being "enjoyed by everyone. These local appearances, plus the many off-campus concerts that they played, were all of a caliber that made us proud that this was our band."

Toward the end of the football season in the fall of 1956, the Tech Wonder Boys and Arkansas State Indians faced off in the Aluminum Bowl played in War Memorial Stadium in Little Rock. In the midst of a rainstorm the two teams played what might be described more aptly as a Mud Bowl, while their respective bands took to the field at halftime and marched a combined show, which included a salute to the NAIA as shown below. The game was played live on the CBS television network. Ironically, the same weather befell the Wonder Boys and the A&M Boll Weevils the following year in the Rice Bowl played in Stuttgart—it was nicknamed the "Mud Bowl of 1957." From the fall of 1955 through the fall of 1957 Austin Lovell served as drum major of the Tech Band.

The Arkansas Tech Alpha Tau colonies of Kappa Kappa Psi and Tau Beta Sigma National Honorary Band Fraternity and Sorority, respectively, became full-fledged chapters in the spring of 1958. The charter members of both chapters are pictured above. (Author's note: Taking personal privilege here, I would like to point out my high school band director, who was also an excellent trombonist—Perry Hope, third from right in the men's photo.)

Although it is difficult to see in the bottom photo, the 1958 Tech Band led by drum major Bill Shryock has outlined the state of Arkansas on the field. The school was celebrating its fiftieth anniversary with the majorettes holding up the names of the four colleges that got their start by Act 100 passed by the Arkansas General Assembly in the spring of 1909. At the time they went by the names of Arkansas Polytechnic College in Russellville or Arkansas Tech, Arkansas State College in Jonesboro or A-State, Arkansas Agricultural and Mechanical College in Monticello or Arkansas A&M, and Southern State College in Magnolia or Southern State. The bus photo indicates the mode of transit for the Arkansas Tech Band in 1958–59 whether it was traveling to away football games in the fall or on a concert tour in the spring.

Loren Bartlett
Director

The above photo of the 1959–60 Esquires dance band reflects the group that had been directed for the past few seasons by Loren Bartlett. Bartlett would leave the campus at the end of the school year and return in the fall of 1961 to the Tech faculty as woodwind instructor with his doctorate in hand. The group was more popular than ever for all kinds of social occasions across the state. One member of the Esquires was Jan Shaw (*first row right*), who later became Director of Bands at SAU in Magnolia. The Concert Band that year was eighty-five members strong and included with their on-campus presentations a northwest Arkansas tour terminating in Fort Smith with a performance at the Bi-State Music Festival. In the fall of 1960 Jack Wood led the Tech Band onto the field for halftime performances in formations like the one below. Note that the football team won the AIC Championship in back-to-back seasons in 1960 and 1961, while the basketball Wonder Boys three-peated the AIC crown in 1960, 1961, and 1962.

Among the highlights of the 1961–62 Tech Concert Band season was the appearance of famed saxophone soloist, Fred Hemke (*above*), in an on-campus concert playing the classic, "Sonata in G Minor" and the modern "Divertimento for Saxophone." For the 1962–63 school year the Arkansas Tech Brass Choir (*shown below*) made its debut on campus under the direction of Don Owen, also the newest director of the Esquires dance band. The Tech Concert Band received the high honor of being invited to participate in the Music Educators National Conference in St. Louis.

The above photos illustrate the 1963–64 Arkansas Tech Marching Band and the majorette line that fronted the group. It was stated in the 1964 *Agricola* that "the band presented 'gridiron stereo' which was first introduced by the Tech Band four years ago. Another first for the band was the presentation of a 'symphonic band sound on the march.'" And new to the staff was Robert Bright, who became the new brass instructor and director of the Esquires and the Brass Choir. During the summer of 1964 Witherspoon conducted the first of the famed Arkansas Tech Band Camps for the benefit of secondary school students. Below, 1964–65 drum major Jearl Mars demonstrates his twirling ability during a football halftime show, and Gene Witherspoon directs the Pep Band in a pep rally to ready the Wonder Boys for yet another game. The football team successfully won the AIC crown at the end of the 1964 season undefeated in the conference and posting a 9–1 overall record.

The 1965–66 Tech Band was invited in March to perform at the MENC (Music Educators National Conference) National Convention in Kansas City, Kansas. Band members were able to wear newly arrived uniforms for the occasion as can be seen in the above photo. The band numbered eighty members that year. Below is a photo of the 1966–67 band consisting of ninety musicians, specially invited to represent the South at the silver anniversary of the College Band Directors National Association Convention in Ann Arbor, Michigan. The event was held in February in the midst of a record snowfall for the area (36–40 inches). That same year Tech's Brass Choir performed at the MENC Convention. Drum major Jerry Boseman and majorettes Jill Witherspoon (*kneeling*), Euna Tirk, Linda Britt, and Gerry Birkhead fronted the 1966 marching band.

The 1967–68 Arkansas Tech Band (*above left*), dubbed as being "Arkansas' Band of Distinction," had an enrollment of 105 students, of which 75 were mentioned in the *Agricola* as having been all-state band students in high school. At right, Director Witherspoon watches the football action on the field. Celebrations were in order for the football team in both 1967 and 1968 as the football team won back-to-back AIC Championships. The 1968–69 Tech Band (*below*), led by drum major Scott Clark, marches at halftime on campus. The band made another appearance at the MENC national convention in the spring at St. Louis.

Tech's "Band of Distinction" started the 1969–70 season heading up a parade down Garrison Avenue in Fort Smith before the Tech–Abilene Christian game played on "neutral" turf (*top photo above*). The football season ended with the band in Little Rock supporting the team against Arkansas AM&N followed by the band's performance at the ASBDA Convention held in Hot Springs in December. Although the basketball Wonder Boys did not win the AIC, the team was invited to the NAIA tournament. The second photo above depicts Witherspoon with the band's percussion section waiting for a cue to begin taping of a program to be broadcast from the studios of AETN in Conway. The photo below right shows drum major John Linder marching through the ranks of the 1970–71 Tech Band during a halftime show precision drill at home. The other photo is evidence that the Pep Band enjoys its role supporting the basketball Wonder Boys.

For the 1971–72 Arkansas Tech Band and the rest of the Fine Arts curriculum on the campus, it was a watershed year with the completion and opening of the new Witherspoon Hall, with the entire Fine Arts Division finally under one roof. Obviously, the building was named for the longtime head of the Division and director of the "Band of Distinction." The photos above are of the band marching in the 1971 Homecoming Parade and drum major Don Hall. Below is the Tech Concert Band of 1972–73 presenting a concert in the new auditorium in Witherspoon Hall. It is worthy to note that the Wonder Boys football teams of both 1970 and 1971 brought home the AIC Championship trophies.

The 1973–74 Arkansas Tech Symphonic Band (*above*) was invited for another appearance before the College Band Director National Association Convention in the spring of 1974 in Houston, Texas. By this time a Russellville Community Orchestra had been going strong for a few years, practicing on the Tech campus and including both Tech students and area residents who wished to play in an instrumental group that included strings. Tech professor Joan Wainwright was the conductor. The twirling line for the 1973 "Band of Distinction" included (*left to right*) Sam Brooks, Elaine Watkins, Sherry Swain, and Nat Conner. The Tech Band's newly added flag line for the fall of 1974 is shown below. Leading the band that season was drum major Steve Workman.

The Tech Band of 1975–76 is shown above left playing in the stands at a home game, while the majorettes of that year are shown posing for the photographer of the *Agricola*. The year 1976 proved to be momentous for Arkansas Tech because it attained university status by the authority of the Arkansas Board of Higher Education effective July 9, 1976. Below are the Jazz Ensemble for 1976–77 and the "Band of Distinction" for that same year posed on their home field. Witherspoon turned over the duties of the marching band that year to Dr. Robert Casey, but "Chief" Witherspoon remained as head of the Music Department.

One hundred and eighteen members of the 1977–78 Arkansas Tech Marching Band are present in the above picture for the school's yearbook photo opportunity. About the same number also performed in the next year's marching unit when the band took the field under the leadership of drum major Randy Rushing (*below left*). The saddest news of the 1978–79 school year for the campus was the death of its longtime chair of the Music Department and beloved band director, Gene "Chief" Witherspoon. He died of a massive heart attack on January 14, 1979, and a standing-room-only crowd attended his memorial service held in the auditorium of Witherspoon Hall on the Tech campus.

Hal Cooper, an experienced band director on the secondary level, was hired to begin in the fall of 1979 as the new Arkansas Tech band director. The picture above left catches the 1979–80 "Band of Distinction" accompanying the Golden Girls dance squad as they perform during a halftime show that fall. The 130-member 1980–81 marching squad, including the saxophone players below, was under the field direction of drum major Charles Dunlap. Also shown is the 1980–81 Symphonic Band that performed a concert for the Arkansas Music Educators Association Convention in Pine Bluff in the spring.

In addition to the drum major and majorettes, the Golden Girls, and the flag line, a new group was added to the "Band of Distinction" in 1979 with the six-member rifle team. The 1982–83 rifle team is shown above along with a press-box view of the whole Tech Marching Band in action during a halftime show that season. The band also presented a show that fall honoring former Tech student, Elizabeth Ward, who was crowned Miss America in September. The record-number 140-member 1982–83 Tech Band is shown below with drum majors Susan McIntyre and Brad Slaten kneeling down front. Note also the record-number fourteen majorettes in the picture. In June 1983 the Tech Symphonic Band performed the final concert of the national convention of the American Band Directors Association meeting in Hot Springs.

The photos above show both the 1983–84 Arkansas Tech Marching Band and the Tech Symphonic Band in action. In 1984 the Wonder Boys basketball team won the AIC Championship for the first time since 1972 under new coach John Widner. In February 1984 the newly formed Wind Ensemble performed for the Arkansas Music Educators Association in Pine Bluff featuring tuba soloist Andy Anders. For the fall of 1984 the Tech Band (*below*) sported new uniforms with green coats and white trousers, while the flag line donned panama hats and gold vests. As usual, the twirlers wore lots and lots of gold sequins. Drum majors were Sally Shedd and Brad Slaten. Also shown below is the Jazz Band performing under the watchful eye of Hal Cooper. In April 1985 the Wind Ensemble played a two-day tour of western Arkansas and the Tulsa area. The program featured Philip Parker, percussion professor, and Dr. Robert Casey as guest conductor.

The 110-member 1985–86 Arkansas Tech Band performed the above precision drill routine as one of the many formations it created during halftime of all the home football games played in Russellville. The group was led on the field by Jon Ladd and Sally Shedd at right. On March 9, 1986, the Symphonic Band was joined by the Arkansas Brass Consort and Arkansas composer laureate Dr. W. Francis McBeth in a major concert on campus. Over the years McBeth frequently visited the Tech Band to read his new works and manuscripts before publication.

Below is the 1986–87 edition of the "Band of Distinction" marching down Russellville's Main Street during the Homecoming Parade and flutist Cindy Irman playing her part in the Homecoming halftime show. On October 28 and November 1 the Tech Band marched exhibition shows at high school marching contests in Russellville and in Little Rock, respectively. In March 1987 the band was chosen to perform for the dedication of the Vietnam Veterans Memorial in Little Rock on the capitol grounds.

The 1987–88 ATU "Band of Distinction" is shown above playing the school fight song in the stands at a home game. Above right is the 1987 band's majorette lineup. Although the Wonder Boys did not see a lot of success on the gridiron in the early to mid-1980s, the roundballers won the 1988 AIC Championship with a 14–4 record and posting 22–11 overall. Below is the photo from the 1989 *Agricola* of that year's ATU Marching Band with drum majors Stacy Tucker and Nena Nance in the middle foreground. The percussionists below are performing during a halftime show in the fall of 1988. In February 1989 Dr. Gary Hill, professor of music at Kansas City Conservatory, guest conducted the Symphonic Band on Ingolf Dahl's *Sinfonitta*.

The photos above reflect both the marching and concert aspects of the 1989–90 ATU "Band of Distinction." Drum majors for the marching season were Brian Greenlear and Cheri Johns. In the spring of 1990 there were two performance bands, the Symphonic Band directed by Hal Cooper and the Concert Band conducted by Dr. Robert Casey. The Symphonic Band was selected to perform at the Southwest Region College Band Directors Association Convention in Norman, Oklahoma. Hal Cooper (*below left*) can be seen directing the 1990–91 Tech Band on the field from the sidelines. Most marching band rehearsals took place during the week on the campus parking lot next to the Corley Building. In February 1991 the Symphonic Band performed a concert for the All-State Convention in Pine Bluff featuring faculty soloists Karen Futterer, Ken Futterer, and Barbara Rentschler on flute, oboe, and clarinet, respectively.

The 1991–92 marching "Band of Distinction" shown above and the Symphonic Band both had multiple venues to show their talent throughout the year. The latter played at the Southwest District of College Band Directors National Association in Fayetteville in January and at the Music Educators National Conference in April in New Orleans. The photos below show the 1992–93 ATU Marching Band performing shows in both War Memorial Stadium (*at left*) and on the home campus football field. Since the ATU Bands support the school's athletic teams, an update on those is as follows: Although the football team had little to crow about between 1988 and 1993, the Wonder Boys basketball team had winning seasons from 1988 through 1997 with AIC Championship seasons in 1993, 1994, and 1995 and a NAIA Final Four appearance in 1995. And the women's team—the Golden Suns—had consecutive winning seasons every season after their first in 1977 through 2003, winning the AIC or Gulf South titles nineteen times. Now that was a team to enjoy playing the fight song for over and over and over . . .

The photos above capture 1993–94 ATU band members practicing their precision drill routines on the campus football field. As in years past, the "Band of Distinction," under the direction of Hal D. Cooper, participated in a number of exhibition marching shows and area parades in addition to performing at football halftime shows. The below left Homecoming 1994 photo shows the ATU Band joined by that fall's Alumni Band in the stands in support of the Wonder Boys, whereas the photos center and right feature a few ATU majorettes and brass players performing on the field. In February 1995 the ATU Symphonic Band performed for the Arkansas All-State Convention in Pine Bluff and was joined by the U.S. Army Brass Quintet from Washington, D.C.

The year 1994 was a bright spot in the Wonder Boys' otherwise dismal football stretch from 1991 through 1998. Not only was 1994 the only year during that time that the team had a winning season, they also won the AIC crown and earned a spot in the NAIA play-offs.

For the 1995–96 school year the ATU band included the majorette unit shown above right and drum majors Cody Gifford and Kim Allen. On March 2, 1996, ATU's Symphonic Band played for the College Band Directors National Association Convention in Wichita, Kansas. In time for the 1996 marching season the 160-member ATU Band acquired the newly distinctive white-jacketed uniforms seen on the drummers and wind instrument players below. Attire was a bit more informal for basketball games played in Tucker Coliseum. The Brass Choir director for the 1996–97 year was Gary Barrow (*at right in center picture below*).

The collage of photos above is from the 1998 *Agricola* yearbook depicting the 1997–98 ATU Marching Band. Also in the yearbook is an article written by David Wesly about director Hal Cooper's love for jazz and his commitment to his music students at the school. Pictured below are members of the 1998–99 "Band of Distinction" and a couple of performers in the Jazz Band. In March of 1999 the Symphonic Band recorded a new compact disk entitled *Songs and Dances.*

The 1999–2000 ATU Marching Band presented a patriotic themed halftime show for the last football game of the season with a finale including the unfurling of the large flag shown above while the band played "America the Beautiful." During the spring the Symphonic Band under the direction of Hal Cooper performed at the dedication ceremonies of the new Ross Pendergraft Library and Technology Center. Below, the 2000–2001 edition of the "Band of Distinction" is on display with the drum line entering Buerkle Field on campus and later with brass players forming the run-through formation for the football team. Homecoming 2000 was notable for its grand celebration honoring fifty years of the "Band of Distinction." Drum majors for the season were Ralph Brody and Leah Sherman.

ATU Fight Song

Fight on, Arkansas Tech,
Fight on to victory!
Break through to run up the score,
Conference Champions once more!
Fight! Fight! Fight!
We'll back you all the way,
Cheering for triumph always!
Go! Fight! Green and Gold!
Wonder Boys, You're Number One!!!

For the 2001-02 marching season Matt McGinty and Leah Sherman (*pictured above*) served as drum majors of the ATU "Band of Distinction." They led the band onto Buerkle Field at the beginning of each home game followed by the majorettes and color guard. The lower right photo above records the band's Homecoming "Blue's Brothers" halftime presentation with brass members playing to the upper seats of the stands. For the third year in a row the Wonder Boys football team had a winning season with an 8–2 record for the fall of 2001. In March 2002 the Symphonic Band was invited to play for the American Bandmasters Association National Convention in Wichita, Kansas. Below are photos of the 2002–03 ATU Band at a football game and in rehearsal. The photo below left shows the band in communal support of a young man's attempt to propose marriage to a female member of the band.

Above are photos of the 2003–04 Pep Band in action at a Wonder Boys basketball game and the marching unit on the ATU gridiron spelling out the traditional pregame "T" through which the football team entered the field. Drum majors Jeremy Wilhelmi and Veronica Lanier are shown on the near sideline and Mark Harris is featured in the photo at right. In the spring of 2004, current members and alumni of the Tech Band threw a surprise party for Hal Cooper at the Russellville Country Club in celebration of his twenty-fifth anniversary as Director of Bands at ATU. Below are photos of the "Band of Distinction" for 2004–05 taken at halftime during the ATU–UAM game (*upper right*), the saxophones in motion during another game (*bottom right*), and what the Russellville newspaper, the *Courier*, dubbed as "Hal's Horns" (*left*) performing in concert. Veronica Lanier and Dustin Summey served as drum majors for the year.

Pictured at right is the 2005–06 ATU Band in the home stands at a fall football game led by drum majors Veronica Lanier and Heather Gordey and above is the Tech Symphonic Band posing on stage in Witherspoon Hall on campus. Notably, the Symphonic Band was chosen to perform for the American School Band Directors Association Convention held in Hot Springs in June 2005. As of this writing there are upwards of 140 in the ATU marching program and 70 in the symphonic band, and Hal Cooper continues as the school's Director of Bands. Tech's intercollegiate athletic program competes in the Division II Gulf South Conference. Arkansas Tech also makes available to its instrumental students a Bachelor of Arts degree in Music and a Bachelor of Music Education degree with an instrumental option.

Arkansas Tech University Alma Mater

Alma Mater, Alma Mater,
May we lift our eyes to thee.
May thy glory and thy honor
Be fore'er our destiny.
May the colors Green and Gold
Our loyal hearts fore'er enthrall,
And thy mem'ry live forever,
In the hearts of us all.

Chapter Six

The Marching Mulerider Band

Southern Arkansas University
Southern State College
Third District Agricultural and
   Mechanical College (Magnolia A&M)
Third District Agricultural School

The current generation of students on the university campus in Magnolia, Arkansas, knows the school by its present name—Southern Arkansas University. Alumni from 1950 to 1976 remember the days when it was known as Southern State College, while earlier graduates from 1925 to 1950 recall its being called the Third District Agricultural and Mechanical College, or more popularly, Magnolia A&M. But before those titles, the school was originally named as one of the four District Agricultural Schools established by the Arkansas General Assembly in 1909 by the passage of Act 100 (refer to the details in the preface). The southwest corner of the state encompassing seventeen counties was designated as the third district, and it was left up to the board of trustees of that district to decide on where to locate the Third District Agricultural School (TDAS).

According to an article written by Mrs. W. M. Jones of the school's English Department and printed in the May 28, 1922, edition of the *Arkansas Gazette,* civic leaders of Magnolia took the lead in procuring the establishment of the school in their town. W. R. Cross, described as "a pioneer citizen of the town," led the charge with the superintendent of public schools J. P. Womack putting on a parade around the town square with students carrying hoes, shovels, bundles of oats and corn, "and many other articles suggestive of a technical school."

Eventually the town bid four hundred acres of land and $44,000 with the backing of the local Peoples Bank and the Columbia County Bank to secure the new school and successfully made the location two miles north of Magnolia the permanent address for the Third District Agricultural School. As with the other three District Agricultural Schools, the Columbia County school was created to be primarily a vocational school emphasizing the teaching of the latest farming techniques and science, the instruction of the mechanical aspects of farm equipment and building construction, plus home economics and food preparation and production. Following the social mores of the time, the first two of the above were directed toward the male students and the last one toward female students. But as the name of the school changed over the years, so did attitudes toward gender abilities and interests evolve over time, as they did on the other Arkansas campuses.

The last of the four District Agricultural Schools to open, the TDAS began classes in January 1911 with its student body made up mostly of preparatory high school students to get them up to par so as to be able to matriculate in the vocational classes. Though there was a heavy emphasis on the agricultural, mechanical, and home economic areas of study at the school, athletics and fine arts were introduced to the campus in its early days. Football was inaugurated at the Magnolia school in 1911, and the Crescendo Music Club in 1914. The latter had as its purpose the creation of a greater interest in music, meeting once a week to "take up the study of some of the great composers, their lives and their works." The photo of the club at the top of the following page appeared in the 1914 TDAS yearbook, the *Monitor.* Also in that year's *Monitor* was the second photo of the school's Cornet Quartet.

The Crescendo Music Club
Motto— "Think twice; play once"
Colors—White and Gold
Flower—Narcissus

The Third District Agricultural School's Crescendo Music Club of 1914.

The TDAS Cornet Quartet, 1913–14 (*clockwise from above left*): Archie Heard, Lee Street, Ira Minton, and Logan Mendenhall.

MUSIC CLASS

MUSICAL RECITAL

PIANO STUDENTS

Unless a student at TDAS had his or her own instrument as did members of the Cornet Quartet on the previous page, participation in instrumental music on the campus was pretty much limited to the piano, and it was basically first come first served at best. Music studies, as a result, in the school's early days was relegated pretty much to music appreciation, teaching techniques, vocal recitals, and occasionally music composition when time allowed for such among the regular curriculum of classes. The above photos (*from the top down*) are the 1914–15 TDAS music appreciation class, the 1915–16 music recital students (a combination of vocal and piano students), and the 1916–17 class of piano students at the TDAS. Note that all three photos were taken against the backdrop of the main building on the campus—the Administration Building.

Until the early 1920s the mascot of all four of the District Agricultural Schools were "the Aggies" since they were all agricultural. But as intercollegiate competition in athletics and other areas heated up early in the century, each school started looking for its own mascot with which to identify. According to E. E. Graham in a paper written called "A Brief History of Southern State College" in recognition of the school's fiftieth anniversary in 1959, this is how the campus attained the "Mulerider" as its mascot:

> Legend has it that the name "Mulerider" originated as a result of a self-sponsored and self-tutored early football team, engaged to play a game with a high school team in a nearby town, and that they rode the college's farm mules as transportation to McNeil to catch a train. No one can be found to vouch for the truth of this story. But it is true, as every farm-raised person of the writer's age in the South knows, that the plow mule played his part as a saddle animal for church and picnic-going for many less privileged farm youth than those who could be more elegantly transported with a saddle horse or in a buggy. Regardless of how many people of the faculty who have joined the staff from city life or sections of the country where the significance of the mule is unknown, the mule and the mulerider are most appropriate as a symbol for the college. At least, that is the writer's opinion.

As early as 1914 the TDAS football team was colloquially called the Muleriders and the yearbook for the 1921–22 year was changed from the *Monitor* to the *Mulerider*. Officially, the football team became the Muleriders in the fall of 1922, and the Mulerider has been the school's mascot ever since.

The first organized instrumental musical organization on the Mulerider campus appears to have occurred in the 1923–24 school year with the above photo of an orchestra printed in the school yearbook. Directed by Mrs. Chester Green the group contained violins, cornets, clarinets, trombones, saxophones, a piano, a banjo, and drums.

During the 1924–25 school year there were both an orchestra and a band on the TDAS campus as illustrated in the above photos with Glen Martel, a graduate of Henderson-Brown, listed as the director of both groups. The band was also part of the National Guard Company at the school; note that the young men are all wearing army uniforms.

Magnolia's vocational school was interchangeably called the Third District Agricultural School and the Third District Agricultural College from its inception until it and its three sister schools were approved by the state legislature in 1925 to become junior colleges called Agricultural and Mechanical Colleges (with the exception of the Second District School which became Arkansas Polytechnic College).

The Third District Agricultural and Mechanical College (more popularly called Magnolia A&M College) displayed its orchestra and band in the 1925–26 *Mulerider* yearbook with the photos shown below. Note that the boys in the band are wearing street clothes, possibly posing for the photographer on a nonmilitary class day.

G. G. Martel, Ph.B.
Mathematics and Music

Football on the Magnolia A&M campus had a regular record from its inception in 1911. The first few years that the school fielded a team, the boys played mostly high schools in south Arkansas, primarily because the Third District campus was essentially a combination preparatory school and vocational technical school. Besides, at the time there were few junior colleges or vo-tech schools with which to compete that also had teams. One or two of the opponents each season were a rival in-state team, however—namely, the A&M school in Monticello or one of the two colleges in Arkadelphia, Henderson and Ouachita. TDAS's greatest era in football was the 1919 season when the team went undefeated 7–0. Magnolia A&M also won the AIC crown three out of the four seasons between 1926–29, and its only opponents were other colleges in and out of state.

The band above left is the 1926–27 Magnolia A&M College Band that played on the sidelines when the Mulerider football team took to the field (note the band's identification on the bass drum head). Partial wear of army uniforms indicates that the band was also officially still part of the school's guard unit. But when it came time for supporting the team, dress and membership of the band became more lax. Close observation will find that there is a female clarinet player among the group. The campus orchestra for the year is shown above right still directed by G. G. (Glen) Martel. No photos of the Third District Band have been found from the following two school years, but the 1927–28 and 1928–29 orchestras are shown below left and right respectively from yearbook photos.

L. E. Crumpler began his tenure with the Magnolia A&M Band in 1929 and served as its director until 1934 (refer to the preface for Crumpler's association with the Martin Bands). His 1929–30 band is shown above with Crumpler standing in the front row right holding a trumpet. Also above right is that year's campus orchestra. Below is the 1930–31 Third District A&M Band with Crumpler again standing in the same position. An interesting sidenote is that the campus orchestra director, G. G. Martel, also played in the band for a number of years and can be seen holding a piccolo in the photo below (*second from left in the front row*). Drum major for that season was Curtiss Youngblood (*extreme left in the front row*). Jimmie Justiss, who was one of Crumpler's assistant directors that year, would become the band's director a few years later.

L. E. Crumpler
Band Director

During the 1931–32 school year there was an additional instrumental group on the Mulerider campus called the String Band made up of violins, banjos, guitars, a mandolin, and a piano (*shown above left*). That year's A&M College Band is shown above right. Look closely behind some of the military-attired young men and you will see some women in the ranks. Obviously at the time, this group was ready to play for a football game.

Football on the Magnolia A&M gridiron was not a winning exercise for the school during the 1930s. In addition to experiencing the decade of the Great Depression, the Muleriders had only a single winning season in that ten-year span—1930—and didn't even field a team from 1937 to 1939. But when the team won, it celebrated. The photo bottom left shows the band leading a contingent of students on a parade around campus after the team beat Arkansas Tech 7–0 in 1932. The 1932–33 Third District Band is also shown below right.

The 1933–34 Magnolia A&M Band shown above right is posed in front of the National Guard Armory Building on campus obviously in preparation for a Military Department activity (the clue: no female members are present). That was Crumpler's last year as the band's director and his assistant was Benjamin Konikoff. The photo above left shows the student soldiers marching southward from the campus toward town followed by the band and, though it is hard to see, a number of students in civilian clothes. The occasion of the event has not been determined, but notice the campus buildings in the background. The administration building is to the left with the two buildings to the right serving as dormitories. Below is the Mulerider Band for 1934–35 with civilian drum major (for sporting events) Virginia Beene standing at attention in the center of the photo. Ben Konikoff took over the director's position from Crumpler for only a single season, assisted by Edward Cross.

Ben Konikoff
Director

Jimmy Justiss
Band Director

J. E. (Jimmy) Justiss became the Third District Band's director in the fall of 1935 and conducted the group until it was disbanded after the 1941–42 school year as a result of America's entering into the war in the Pacific. Justiss is shown above in a rare photo taken of the band in its rehearsal hall within what was known as the "Tin Brick" Building on campus and on the field at halftime performing a show that included the campus spirit melody, "The Loyalty Song." Jimmy Smith was drum major for military events and Novis Taylor was drum major for athletic events. Below is the 1936–37 Magnolia A&M Band directed by Justiss and the school's Dance Orchestra directed by C. E. Haydon. As a point of reference, the Third District A&M School did not accept high school preparatory students in its enrollment after the spring of 1937. Beginning with the fall of 1937 the school was strictly a junior college for the first time.

The photos above show both the Magnolia A&M Band and the Dance Orchestra for the 1937–38 school year with J. E. Justiss directing the former and C. E. Haydon directing the latter. The photos below show the same groups but for the following year 1938–39 with the same men directing. Lawrence Jarnagin served as the marching unit's drum major both years, and local benefactor Elizabeth McMorella and the college's president Charles Overstreet acted as the band's sponsors. Miss McMorella can be spotted to the right of the second row in both group photos.

In the photos above picturing the 1939–40 Third District A&M College Band and the Dance Orchestra, director J. E. Justiss was listed in the *Mulerider* yearbook as the director of both groups and even played saxophone in the orchestra. He is seated in the middle of the front row. Even with World War II sweeping across Europe and North Africa and spreading into the Pacific Ocean, the Magnolia A&M Band still dressed out a healthy number of members as the bottom photo of the 1940–41 group shows. And amazingly enough, most of the musicians pictured are male.

After the bombing of Pearl Harbor on December 7, 1941, most of the country's attention turned to the war effort, and the enrollment of the male population declined on the Magnolia A&M campus as it did across most of the United States. But prior to that "day that will live in infamy," the Third District A&M Band did field a small twenty-nine-member group that played for home football games and even traveled to an away game at Paris Junior College in Texas. The 1941–42 Mulerider Band is shown above marching in a parade through Magnolia streets along with a photo of the newly renamed Varsitonians Dance Orchestra. Director Justiss is in the latter group also but playing a trombone this time. Justiss did not return to the faculty the following school year and football disappeared from the Mulerider campus as an intercollegiate sport for the 1942 through 1945 seasons. Basketball was discontinued at the same time but returned late in the fall of 1945. Note that the Varsitonians Dance Orchestra remained active under student leadership.

In the fall of 1944 instrumental music returned to the Magnolia A&M campus when Dr. J. W. Chadwick, the director of high school bands at Magnolia, Stamps, and Waldo, combined his secondary musicians with interested Third District college students to form the band pictured below. Fifteen students are A&M students and the whole group wore the college's uniforms. Mostly they played for high school sporting events, community parades, and patriotic activities. Chadwick is seated in the dark suit in the front row right.

Loyalty Song
Words by Harriet Kay

Loyalty Song

As the blue and the gold of our banner so bright
Fill our hearts full of joy and pride,
To the A and MC we will always be true
No matter what else may betide.
We have pledged all our love and our loyalty, too,
To maintain the high standards begun.
May the gold never tarnish, the blue ne'er grow dim,
Til the goal of our hopes has been won.

In the fall of 1946 the Magnolia A&M campus was trying to get itself back to a sense of normalcy after the war's end, and in the process hired Adam West, a graduate of Centenary College, to direct the A&M Band, which was still at the time a combined group of Magnolia High School students and the college's students. The 1946–47 marching unit seen above is the result of his efforts. West stayed in that position for only two years, though he is credited with rebuilding efforts in instrumental music on the campus. Below is the 1947–48 Mulerider Band still containing both secondary and college musicians. Drum major Betty Clayton is standing at attention at the right of the photo.

Adam E. West

Richard O. Oliver

In the fall of 1948 Richard O. Oliver joined the Magnolia A&M faculty as the new Director of Bands and remained in that position until the spring of 1972. Oliver, a graduate of the University of Oklahoma with bachelor's and master's degrees, is shown above with his first college concert band and the Mulerider Band on parade around Magnolia's town square. Avis Chambers was the group's drum major for 1948–49. Football made a comeback that year on the campus with the team's claiming a share of the AIC title. Below is the 1949–50 Third District A&M Band and twirlers along with that year's edition of the Varsitonians. Director Oliver is seen playing on trumpet with the latter group next to the trombone player in the back row.

The following paragraph was quoted from the current SAU website:

In the fall of 1949, the Board of Trustees of Magnolia A&M, excercising authority vested in it by the State Legislature, decided to make the college a four-year, degree-granting institution. The Board authorized the adding of third-year college courses to begin with the fall semester of 1950, and fourth-year or senior courses to begin with the fall semester of 1951. By Act Eleven, January 24, 1951, the State Legislature changed the name of the institution to Southern State College.

The above photo of the Magnolia A&M Band was taken in the fall of 1950 prior to the school being renamed Southern State College, and the Fine Arts Building shown above included a band room in which director Oliver is shown rehearsing the group during the 1950–51 school year.

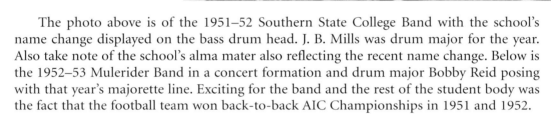

The photo above is of the 1951–52 Southern State College Band with the school's name change displayed on the bass drum head. J. B. Mills was drum major for the year. Also take note of the school's alma mater also reflecting the recent name change. Below is the 1952–53 Mulerider Band in a concert formation and drum major Bobby Reid posing with that year's majorette line. Exciting for the band and the rest of the student body was the fact that the football team won back-to-back AIC Championships in 1951 and 1952.

The 1953–54 Southern State Band is shown above poised in the campus Greek amphitheatre prior to their newly inaugurated Spring Concert Tour which played for high school audiences across the southern part of Arkansas. Also pictured is the newly formed Riderettes, a drill team of campus coeds that sometimes marched in conjunction with the Mulerider Band and then at other times performed routines to the band's accompaniment. Below is the 1955–56 Rider Marching Band making the loop around the Magnolia town square and that year's edition of the Varsitonians in performance at a dance on campus under the direction of Richard Oliver.

Drum major Mary Ann Hooper

Amid holiday street decorations the 1956–57 Southern State Band and Riderettes drill team march through Magnolia's streets in the annual Christmas Parade of 1956. Also shown above is that year's drum major Mary Ann Hooper. Pictured rehearsing in the band room in the Fine Arts Building below is the 1957–58 SSC Concert Band along with a photo of the Mulerider Band and the Riderettes participating in the 1957 Homecoming Parade.

In addition to playing for Mulerider football and basketball games the 1958–59 Southern State Band also played concerts on campus in the auditorium as pictured above. Note that the men wore suits and ties and the women wore long formal gowns—quite a dress-up affair. Also shown above is drum major Janette Fincher with her majorette line that year. The 1959–60 SSC Band with drum major Dona Williams below is seated in a bit less formal arrangement setup while the Varsitonians are shown taking a break from a dance gig on campus.

On this page are photos of the 1960–61 and 1961–62 Southern State College Band (*above and below, respectively*) in what became a stock pose for the annual yearbook picture in front of the band's new home in the recently completed Fine Arts Building. Also shown above are the Varsitonians for 1960–61. Drum major for the SSC Band for the two years represented here and the following two years was Richard Martin.

The 1962–63 SSC Mulerider Band is shown above on the field and in concert in the campus field house under the direction of Richard Oliver. Below the 1963–64 Southern State Band grew to sixty-three in membership, marched at six football games, performed at a number of pep rallies and parades, and played at all the home basketball games in addition to presenting three concerts on campus and taking a spring tour for concerts at high schools in southern Arkansas. The marching unit below is shown performing at the 1963 Homecoming game.

Sponsor
Richard Oliver

During the 1964–65 school year the Southern State Band welcomed to the campus the establishment of chapters of the national Kappa Kappa Psi band service fraternity and the national Tau Beta Sigma band service sorority. The fraternity subtitled its Delta Chi chapter the Crescendo Club, while the sorority subtitled its Gamma Omicron chapter the Marcato Club. Charter members of both groups are pictured above. For the 1965–66 school year the SSC Concert Band shown below filled its concert stage with sixty musicians and presented performances that attracted audiences from all over southwest Arkansas. Drum major for the Marching Muleriders for three years was James Robbins (*shown below right*). Good news for SSC fans on the basketball front was that the team won the AIC Championship in 1966 for the first time since 1952, and then came back and repeated the honor the following year.

During the 1966–67 school year the Southern State Band performed at all the home football games including the one shown above where the Muleriders played the Bison of Harding. The SSC Band is shown standing in the end zone awaiting the conclusion of the Farmerville High School Band's halftime performance (the Farmerville Band marched in the absence of the Harding Band at the game). Also pictured above is Richard Oliver rehearsing the Concert Band for a presentation the following spring. The photos below are of the 1967–68 Marching Mulerider Band and that year's Concert Band performing in their respective venues of the Homecoming Parade and the Spring Concert.

In 1968–69, the SSC Band received new uniforms with tall shako hats that doubled as concert tuxedos when the vest overlays and shoulder cords were removed as reflected in the two photos above. The pictures below present the 1969–70 Rider Band standing at attention on the SSC football field in Wilkins Stadium and in the stands in the field house during a spirited pep rally prior to one of the gridiron contests. Drum major Dudley Coker served in that position for the two years represented on this page.

The 1970–71 school year was the last term that Richard O. Oliver served as Director of Bands at Southern State. He remained on the faculty afterward, teaching music theory courses into the 1980s. His last marching unit was the SSC Band shown above taking to the streets of Magnolia during that season's Homecoming Parade led by drum major Chuck Downey. In the spring of 1971 the Mulerider basketball team brought home the AIC crown. Jan Shaw came to the SSC campus in 1971–72, having been the high school band director at Searcy, and took on the job of directing both the marching and concert bands at the college. He is shown below directing during a rehearsal in the band room along with that year's majorette line displaying their ability to twirl with fire batons.

The 1972–73 Marching Rider Band above leads the Homecoming Parade in the fall and included in its portfolio that year contemporary tunes such as "Jesus Christ Superstar" and songs from the Three Dog Night rock group that were played at football games, pep rallies, and basketball games. Note that the Mulerider football team finished that season as co-champs of the AIC Conference. On balance, the Concert Band, represented by bassoonist Lynn Dix above, performed two concerts on campus and a three-day tour around the state to Arkansas high school audiences. The photos below reflect the 1973–74 Southern State Band on the field in action during a halftime show that year and on the front steps of the Fine Arts Building playing for a pep rally.

Director Jan Shaw added a new element to the SSC Band profile in the 1974–75 school year—the flag line shown above dressed in bright sequins similar to the majorette line. Bob Artebury served his first year as drum major that season. Also pictured above is the SSC Band posing for the *Mulerider* yearbook in a rustic outdoor setting. Arduous rehearsal like that shown below left was reason enough for entertaining halftime shows for the 1975–76 Rider Band on performance nights. That year's majorette line shows that practicing smiles never hurts.

After approval by the Arkansas State Legislature, the campus of Southern State College was officially changed to Southern Arkansas University on July 9, 1976. As a result the reader will notice that the 1976–77 SAU Band above wore uniforms without the familiar "SSC" on their overlays as in years past, and simply wore ones that were void of identification. But the no-name uniforms didn't last long, however, for the next year the band acquired the uniforms below with SAU proudly displayed on the pennant worn off the belt. Also new for the 1977–78 season was a new band director in Kenneth Guthrie pictured below as well as a new rifle corps that joined the existing feature twirler, majorette line (*below*), and flag line. Scott Pollock (*above left*) served as the drum major for both years depicted on this page.

Although the SAU band underwent a downturn in enrollment in the 1978–79 school year, student spirit was still highly supportive of the campus's athletic teams. Joining drum major Scott Pollock in front of the band during the Homecoming and Christmas Parades that year was feature twirler Lisa Hogue shown above, while the above flag line members brought up the rear. Below is the 1979–80 Rider Band on parade with that year's feature twirler Tracy Lewis and members of the rifle corps.

Danny L. Lowe was the new director of the SAU Band program in 1980–81 and is shown above rehearsing the Concert Band for a program on campus that year after football season ended, the latter of which featured halftimes performed by the Rider Band. The flag line is shown preparing for one of those shows. The SAU band grew in size in 1981–82 to that shown below in a pose in front of the Dolph-Camp Fine Arts Building, which housed the band and the rest of the Music Department. Keith Glass served as drum major for the year.

Having come on board as Director of Bands in the spring of 1982, Eddie Epperson guided the 1982–83 Rider Band through the following ten marching and concert seasons (save for the 1990–91 year). Musicians pictured above are parading through Magnolia streets during Homecoming activities in the fall of 1982. Also shown above is drum major Gary Martin directing the band in the stands in a spirited tune to encourage the team and entertain the crowd. For the 1983–84 season Epperson ordered new uniforms styled as cowboy and cowgirl outfits including yellow western chaps. Better images of those uniforms can be seen on following pages. Drum major for the year was Suzie Barnett and former SAU Band director Richard Oliver is shown below guest conducting the band during the Homecoming '83 halftime show. The photo below left is of the SAU Band rehearsing for a concert in the auditorium of the Dolph-Camp Fine Arts Building.

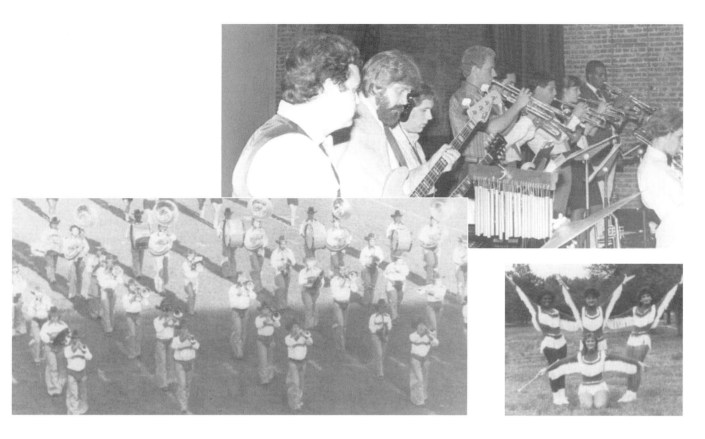

Under the direction of Eddie Epperson, the SAU Band again grew in numbers in 1984–85 and reintroduced the jazz dimension to the music curriculum. Note the chaps on the Marching Rider Band above. Adopting the slogan "The Pride of the South," the 1985–86 Rider Band went through field rehearsals shown below in order to present shows of which they were more increasingly proud. The woman to the left is pounding the bass drum in a ritual called "The Heartbeat of SAU," wherein the drum is continuously beat from the time of the pep rally up until kickoff of the Homecoming game. Epperson was assisted that year by David Chism and David Langford.

Not only was the Marching Rider Band growing in size, but the 1986–87 SAU Concert Band was also adding new members each year under director Eddie Epperson (*shown above left*). Below, the 1987–88 Rider Band is shown in action on the field in Wilkins Stadium during a football halftime show along with Stephanie Day, who served three years as the group's drum major. The year's Concert Band is shown performing a Mother's Day Concert in the campus auditorium.

The Rider Band for 1988–89 was the largest it had ever been, with 109 members on the field and 85 musicians in the Concert Band. The Marching Riders are shown above enduring one of the frequent rainy football games that season. Also shown are members of the SAU Jazz Band under the direction of David Langford and the band's feature twirler LeeAnna Hicklin. Members of the 1989–90 Rider Band are shown below performing during a halftime show as the majorette line poses for a 1990 *Mulerider* yearbook photo.

Beginning in the fall of 1990 James Shearer joined the SAU faculty as the new band director with Eddie Epperson remaining on staff to teach other music courses. The band also received new uniforms for 1990–91, updating their western look. Also pictured above is the Pep Band performing at a Mulerider basketball game in the campus field house. The football team had a successful year culminating with an invitation to play in the Aztec Bowl in Mexico City against the Mexican National All-Star team. SAU won the contest 41–31. Shearer left SAU after one year for a position at New Mexico State, which brought Eddie Epperson back as director of the Marching and Concert Bands. New to the staff in 1991–92 was Dr. Victor Vallo, who assisted Epperson and directed the Jazz Band. The Jazz Band shown below entertained at some of that year's football games as well as doubled as a pep band for the basketball games. Shannon Hensley at right served as drum major for the school year.

For the 1992–93 school year Greg Lisemby took the baton as Director of Bands at SAU, with Dr. Ron Wray signing on as his assistant and director of the Jazz and Pep Bands. The following year with both directors remaining in place the band program continued to build a solid reputation. Below are the 1993–94 SAU Rider Marching Band posing in front of Dolph-Camp Fine Arts Building and the Jazz Band on display in the Fine Arts Auditorium.

Brightening up SAU halftime shows in the 1994–95 school year was the delivery of new uniforms for the Rider Band shown above. That year's Pep Band also pictured above played to lift the morale of the basketball team and fans in the final season of the Arkansas Intercollegiate Conference. The AIC dissolved in the spring of 1995 and most of the former conference teams joined the Gulf South Conference. Below are the 1995–96 Rider Band, the Wind Ensemble, and the Jazz Band. Joining director Greg Lisemby that year was Dr. Allen Buffington, who assisted with the Rider Band and directed the Concert Band and the Jazz Band, while Lisemby took the leadership with the Rider Band and the Wind Ensemble.

The 1996–97 SAU Band above displayed a more casual dress code when it took to the streets during the 1996 Homecoming Parade, but the sound was all business as usual with horns up! Director Greg Lisemby had a strong contingent of musicians on board for the 1997–98 school year as shown in the photos below. The football season was particularly exciting for the Rider Band to play the "Loyalty Song" in that the Muleriders ended the season as co-champions of the Gulf South Conference with a 9–2 record.

J. P. Wilson began his SAU Director of Bands career in 2000 and is still in that position as of this printing. Sarah Mickey, who had held the position as interim director the previous year (and was only the third woman to date to helm a college marching/concert band program in Arkansas), stayed on as Wilson's assistant director and remains so as this book goes to press. Members of the 2000–2001 Rider Band are shown above in informal dress at a football pep rally, in marching uniform during a halftime show and in everyday attire during a rehearsal in the new band hall. Photos of the 2001–02 SAU Band below feature the marching unit during a halftime show and the Jazz Band featuring Kelsey Harell in concert in Harton Theater on campus.

Mulerider Fight Song

We are the Blue and Gold
'Riders so strong and bold
We've got the spirit
Come on, let's hear it!
Shout out for good ol' SAU
GO! GO! GO!
GO 'Riders, go along,
This is our favorite song,
Oh, it's M U L E R I D E R
'Riders, the best of SAU!!!

The 2003–04 edition of the SAU Mulerider Band is shown above left marching through the streets of Magnolia during that year's Homecoming Parade, while industrious flute players practice on the campus lawn. In 2003 Michael Britt was hired as percussion instructor and still serves as director of the Jazz program as of this writing. Below, the band plays for a televised pep rally as cheerleaders perform acrobatic stunts before an alumni crowd. Also pictured is the Mulerider mascot, who proudly races the length of the football field with school flag in hand after each team score (the school participates in the Division II Gulf South Conference).

The 2004–05 SAU Mulerider Band led by drum majors Alicia Covington and Eric Keener above played for a pregame celebration with the football team's cheerleaders and SAU president Dr. David Rankin in the gathering area outside the home stadium. Current Direct of Bands J. P. Wilson is pictured above right. And below, the 2005–06 SAU Band is shown in rehearsal and in performance during the final home game of the season in Wilkins Stadium against Henderson State University. The band, led by drum majors Eric Keener and Al Torres, marched one hundred musicians that fall and alternated between wearing white and black trousers for shows. For the last show, the seniors wore white trousers while the rest of the band wore black ones as can be seen in the photos below.

Finally, as this book was going to press, preparations were being made on a groundbreaking ceremony in the early fall of 2006 for the construction of a new band building on the SAU campus. Degree programs available to undergraduate band students continue to include a Bachelor of Music Education and a Bachelor of Arts in Music.

Chapter Seven

The Pride of Southeast Arkansas

University of Arkansas at Monticello
Arkansas Agricultural and Mechanical College
Fourth District Agricultural and Mechanical School
Fourth District Agricultural School

As were the current Arkansas universities that are located in Jonesboro, Russellville and Magnolia, the University of Arkansas at Monticello had its beginnings as a District Agricultural School. When the Arkansas General Assembly passed the bill creating these four schools in 1909 (see the preface for more details), Monticello was chosen as the southeast Arkansas location for the Fourth District Agricultural School as a result of some intense lobbying by local entrepreneurs and politicians. With each of the schools having had a board of trustees appointed by the state's governor, each board was responsible to set forth the procurement of the land necessary for such an institution and the building program needed to benefit its future students. The Fourth District School's trustees worked through the process whereby the people of Drew County in which Monticello is located donated two hundred acres initially on which to establish the new school and provided $40,200 through the Drew County Bank to erect its first buildings.

Following through with their pledge for the school, the Fourth District Agricultural School opened its doors on September 14, 1910, to serve its first group of students and has been in operation without interruption to this day. Of course, there have been many changes on the campus and in its course of instruction through the years as there have been at the other colleges and universities in the state. But the location of the campus is still where it originally was established, and the school's story is no less interesting than its counterparts.

Remembering that all the Agricultural Schools were created initially for the education of farmers as to the most advanced and profitable means to enhance their farm work, plus the maintenance of machinery and the training for home management and economics, the emphasis on the arts did not have the highest priority for the administration and trustees in the beginning. But in 1910 Superintendent J. L. Spence oversaw a faculty that was listed in that year's catalog as including a "Directress of Music, Piano and Voice," a teacher of piano and harmony, and a director of band and orchestra. The latter's name was Otto Mahling, who had studied at both the Conservatory of Berlin and the Conservatory of Vienna.

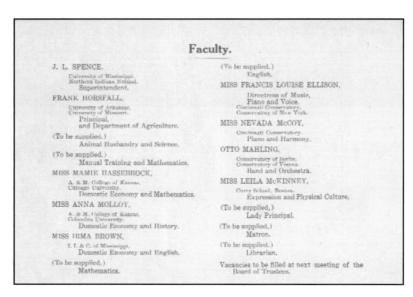

The above is a facsimile of the faculty page from the Fourth District Agricultural School's 1910 catalog.

Otto Mahling was listed as being the instrumental director at the school through the 1913 catalog. From that time until the end of World War I there appears not to have been a band on the Fourth District School's campus. Sometime in the early 1920s a railroad man by the name of C. A. Wallick was transferred to Monticello to work in the town's depot. Having directed the National Guard's 153rd Infantry Band in Little Rock for the duration of World War I, Wallick extended his musical interest in Monticello by directing the Monticello town band and that of the Fourth District School. Wallick's son, Lee Wallick, was off at school up North during that time and later became a professional string bass musician in Chicago. In 1924, when the elder Wallick was transferred to El Dorado, Lee was called by his father to come down to Monticello and take over his bands, including a new town band he had started in Warren.

In the 1925 *Boll Weevil* yearbook there are the photos shown above indicating that there was a band and orchestra on the A&M campus that year (the state legislature had changed the name of the school to Arkansas Agricultural and Mechanical College with junior college status). Lee Opha Wallick is pictured standing behind the drum in the orchestra photo and to the extreme right in the band photo. According to the school's internet website, "UAM's early students, most of them the sons and daughters of delta cotton planters, selected the Boll Weevil as their mascot in admiration of its toughness and the fear it caused among farmers. It's been said that the Boll Weevil is the only thing tough enough to ever truly lick the South."

In the 1929 yearbook the above photos were found which included names of all the players and identified the director of the orchestra as being Horace Adams. Although the photos are not the sharpest for viewing, the smaller photo shows nine of the male members of the group dressed up in costume to march in the school's Homecoming Parade. The photo below is of the 1931–32 A&M College Orchestra, primarily a dance band still directed by saxophonist Horace Adams.

In the late 1920s and early 1930s Lee O. Wallick was a prolific band builder. He started school and town bands all across the southern portion of Arkansas and directed as many as six bands at the same time itinerating from town to town. But his longest gig was at Arkansas A&M from 1924 to 1951. In 1935 while serving as a Monticello volunteer firefighter, Wallick lost his sight in an accident when a board fell on his head during a fire. But he never let it slow him down. Not only was he a director of many bands, he also became the owner/operator of a number of Wallick Music Stores across Arkansas and Mississippi. Lee O. Wallick is shown in a light suit in both of the above photos of the A&M Girls' Drum Corps and the A&M Band in 1932–33. The drum major for the band was listed as Burns Bennett. The photo below is the 1934–35 A&M Band with Clayton Hanson serving as drum major.

The photos on this page reflect the diversity of the instrumental music program on the Arkansas A&M campus during the 1935–36 school year. The top group shot is of the newly renamed Girls' Drum and Bugle Corps because the bugle players were added that year. Both the Corps and the regular A&M Band were directed by Lee Wallick and both sported large bass drums proudly proclaiming the Aggie moniker. The third photo shows the band marching around the Monticello town square leading a group of students in a pep rally, while the remaining photo features the campus's dance band orchestra, "The Southerners," continuing under the direction of Horace Adams but now listed as Dr. Horace Adams.

Lee Wallick, *Band Director*

The 1936–37 Arkansas A&M Aggie Band is shown above posing with the Girls' Drum and Bugle Corps in front of the school's main building on campus. The band also marched that year in parades and performed concerts in Crossett, Stuttgart, England, Warren, Fordyce, Conway, and Little Rock, Arkansas, and in Cleveland, Mississippi. At the time, the Arkansas A&M Band was the largest college band in the state and was led on the field by drum majors Joe Willis, Mildred Ellis, and Cora Cook; Mutt Wall served as drum major of the drum and bugle corps. Also shown above is the Southerners Dance Band, which was alternately directed by Dr. Horace Adams and Jack Shelton.

Wallick's 1937–38 A&M Band is shown above in their red and black uniforms as members are shown playing in the football stands, standing at attention on the field and sitting in concert formation before arches familiar to college alumni. Leading the band were drum majors Jack Shelton, Anice Brock, and Jo Hutchinson. Also pictured is the popular Southerners Dance Band clad in white sports coats and directed by Jack Shelton. Below is the 1938–39 Arkansas A&M Band led by drum major Maxine Scott.

With the Great Depression in the rear-view mirror and the world gearing up for World War II, the Arkansas A&M campus in the fall of 1939 was bustling with student activity, and the various branches of the Aggie band program were full of students playing with enthusiasm. The Drum and Bugle Corps above was supervised by Lee Wallick, but the brass instruction was the responsibility of student Edward Saunders, while the percussion was directed by student Fred Schneider (*standing left and right, respectively, in the top right photo*). The drum majors of the A&M Marching Band above were Maxine Scott and Cotham Rial.

A notation in the 1940 *Boll Weevil* yearbook states that regarding the concert band "Mr. Wallick presents the band to the public twice monthly with a complete change of program, varying the concerts by combining classical and popular music. The band prides itself by being able to master the hardest marches and the deepest overtures, but at the same time the ability to crop their long hair and swing it." By that time the dance band was calling itself "The Collegians" and the band's maestro, Jack Shelton, had his initials on the front of each musician's music stand.

Lee O. Wallick, *Director*

By the end of the 1940–41 school year the Arkansas A&M campus was starting to see some of its enrollment drop due to young men entering the military and the Aggie Band's roster reflected this drop in its group shot above. The dance band was still at full steam, though its directorship changed at semester from Jack Shelton to Leslie Shipley. The Drum and Bugle Corps was as popular as ever.

The A&M Band's last grouping prior to America's official entry into the war in the Pacific Theater after the bombing of Pearl Harbor was the 1941–42 edition of the band shown above in marching and concert formation and the Girls' Drum and Bugle Corps that marched at Boll Weevil football games in the fall of 1941. After that school year the band program was put on hold on the Aggie campus and was not resumed until after the war ended. Lee Wallick concentrated on directing the Monticello and Warren High School Bands and substituted for the band director from Dumas High School who had entered the military. But band music would actually return to the A&M campus before the war ended.

In 1943 the U.S. Navy established on the Arkansas A&M campus a Navy V-12 unit to train recruits in various tasks before being sent off to wartime posts. Included in those military men were a number of well-trained musicians who eventually fell under the baton of the college's own Lee O. Wallick. The V-12 men performed a number of concerts during their stay on the campus, but the band roster routinely changed due to the constant rotation in and out of soldiers. The unit pulled out from A&M shortly after the war ended in 1945.

Wallick attempted to resume the band program at Arkansas A&M in the school year 1945–46 and, by the fall of 1946, the above band was again marching on the campus, and the stage band shown above, Richard Coke and His Orchestra, was swinging down the lane in the spring of 1947. The woman playing saxophone in the front row was Betty Sue Fikes, one of Wallick's students who eventually became his "eyes" and longtime chauffeur. The photo below is of the 1948–49 A&M Aggie Boll Weevil Band.

The 1949–50 Arkansas A&M Band is shown above, as is that year's dance orchestra, once again taking on the name "The Collegians" (interestingly enough, the reader will notice that other college dance bands in the state adopted that same name). The sax player to the extreme right in the front row is Homer Brown, who would become a legendary band director at Arkansas State Teachers College in Conway (today UCA).

Over the years Lee Wallick developed a heart problem, which only got worse, forcing him to retire from Arkansas A&M at the end of the school year 1950–51. But he still helmed the Monticello High School Band, supervised his Wallick Music Stores, and helped run the summer Dixie Music Camps created in 1938 for the benefit of secondary school musicians. Wallick's last A&M Marching Band is shown below with his directing the group in the National Anthem and John Comer serving as his drum major (*center front*). The second photo is of the Concert Band performing under his direction during an outdoor spring campus concert.

Mr. A. A. Harris
Director

Taking the baton from Wallick in the fall of 1951 was A. A. Harris, who led the A&M Band in performances at home Aggie football games, at the away game against Little Rock Junior College played in Pine Bluff, and for the Homecoming Parade in Monticello. The Concert Band played concerts in the on-campus Armory, sometimes in conjunction with the A&M Chorus. Also above is the 1951–52 A&M Dance Band. The 1952–53 Aggie Dance Band is shown below along with the building on the campus that housed both the A&M Band and art classes.

The 1953–54 Arkansas A&M Band and Dance Orchestra are shown above along with the school's alma mater (only the first verse is normally used). Joe Kendricks, one of the snare drum players in the above photo, was that year's drum major. In the fall of 1954 the A&M Band found itself with another new band director in Fred Bellott (*standing to the extreme right in the dance band photo below*). Band Days, which were becoming more popular across the South as recruiting events for college bands of high school band students, came to the A&M campus for Homecoming 1954 as shown below.

Quincy Hargis
*Band Director and Instructor
of Instrumental Music*

For the school year 1955–56 the Arkansas A&M Band acquired another new director in Quincy Hargis, who most recently had received his Master's in Education degree from LSU. His band and twirling line for that year are shown above. The drum major, Frances Thompson in the dark uniform, served in that position for four marching seasons beginning with 1955. Below are the 1956–57 Aggie Band and that year's version of the high school invitational Band Day.

174 ᴀ+ᴍ's Dance Band the ArisTocraTs

At the end of the 1957–58 football season Arkansas A&M capped its fourth straight year as the AIC Champions and played Arkansas Tech in the newly created Rice Bowl, an event specifically established for small colleges. On December 2 in Stuttgart, the Wonder Boys beat the Boll Weevils 20–7 in what was more like a cold, wet, and dreary "Mud Bowl." The photos above are of the 1957–58 Aggie Band, the campus Dance Band (now the Aristocrats), and that year's majorette line. The little girl in the foreground is director Hargis's daughter Sally, who was the band's mascot and dressed out with the band during the fall seasons of 1956 through 1959. Below is pictured the 1958–59 Arkansas A&M Band.

The 1959–60 Aggie Band is shown above in its last year under the direction of Quincy Hargis. Also pictured is the Pep Band that traveled to football games, which the whole band was unable to attend. The band is shown above right led by drum major Gerrye Smith marching in the 1959 Homecoming Parade through the streets of Monticello. Below is the 1960–61 Arkansas A&M Band led onto the field by drum major Searcy Thomas. Also shown is the new director, Wayne K. "Pop" Wilson, directing the band in the stands at a football game.

Wayne K. Wilson
Director

Terry Garrett is shown above serving as drum major for the 1961–62 Arkansas A&M Band along with that year's majorette line and Jackie Bass (*sitting on ground*) in her first of four seasons as the band's feature twirler. The 1962–63 Boll Weevil Band below represented the A&M campus in that fall's Arkansas Livestock Show Parade in Little Rock. The A&M Dance Band played for many of the on-campus dances as well as the All College Beauty Pageant in the spring.

The 1963–64 Arkansas A&M Band is pictured above going through one of the marching routines that was performed at a game on campus, on a road trip to the Sight Bowl in Pine Bluff or at the ASTC game played in Conway. The Concert Band occasion above is the Mid-Winter Concert presented in the on-campus Armory. Members of the 1964–65 Aggie Band are shown below posing for a *Boll Weevil* yearbook photo and playing in the home stands for a football game. Gail M. Campbell, with a Master's degree in Music Education from North Texas State University, was the new director for the Aggie Band that year, and Dick Reynolds was listed as being the group's drum major.

Gail Campbell, *director*

Under Gail Campbell the Aggie Band grew in size and is shown above marching in the Arkansas Livestock Show Parade in the fall of 1965. In addition to traveling to a number of the away football games and playing at home basketball games, the Aggie Band also marched in the Dumas and Pine Bluff Christmas Parades and the Drew County Fair Parade. The 1965–66 Aggie Concert Band, also shown above, went on a spring tour of southeast Arkansas high schools. As in most years, the photo below left shows the mode of travel for the Aggie Band in 1966–67. By this time, the Aggie Band had tagged itself "The Sound of the Delta," sporting new uniforms and adding a new assistant band director for Gail Campbell, Gerald Grant. That year's majorettes are also pictured below.

Gail Campbell took on a new assistant director for 1967–68 with Dennis Vaughan and directed the Aggie Band in the Drew County Fair Parade in Monticello, the Southeast Arkansas Livestock Parade in Pine Bluff, and the State Livestock Exposition Parade in Little Rock in addition to the Mardi Gras Parade in New Orleans. The A&M Band for that year is shown above with its twirling unit. The following year Dennis Vaughan moved up to the director's position and the band's slogan changed from "Sound of the Delta" to "Spirit of A & M." Vaughan is pictured below with the 1968–69 Arkansas A&M Band and majorette line with drum major Gloria Williams positioned in the center.

The images above are of the 1969–70 Arkansas A&M Marching and Concert Bands. The left photo shows the band marching past the state capitol building in Little Rock during the Arkansas Livestock Exhibition Parade, and the right photo was taken in concert performance on-campus with Dennis Vaughan directing. The national band service fraternity, Kappa Kappa Psi, found a place on the Monticello campus when a chapter was installed at the school in 1970–71; its charter members are shown below left. Also shown are the Marching Aggie Band during the Drew County Fair Parade and the Concert Band posing for a photograph in that year's *Boll Weevil* yearbook. James E. Dunlap, who had joined the staff as the band's woodwind instructor the previous year, took over as the A&M director in 1970–71.

The image above left was taken during the 1971–72 marching season of the Boll Weevil Band, while the photo above right was taken during the 1972–73 season. Note that the overlays on the band uniforms reflect the fact that Arkansas A&M became part of the University of Arkansas System, and therefore underwent a name change to the University of Arkansas at Monticello and the initials UAM. The photo below left printed in the 1974 *Boll Weevil* yearbook is of James Nelson King Jr., a beloved Aggie Band and Choir member known as "Big Bill," who died during the 1973–74 school year; he was described as "a legend in his own time." Also shown below are charter members of the UAM chapter of the national band service sorority, Tau Beta Sigma, and the UAM Concert Band for 1973–74.

The James Dunlap-directed A&M Band for 1974–75 is shown above in the home stands behind a sign painted by the band's Kappa Kappa Psi chapter indicating support for the "Mean Green" football team. The Concert Band for the year is also shown above. As was usual for other Arkansas campuses during the 1975–76 school year, a common theme for halftime shows and concerts was the United States Bicentennial celebration which can be seen in the bottom photo of that year's A&M Concert Band. Also pictured is the 1975–76 Marching Boll Weevils majorette line with Becky Nichols (*center*) serving as drum major.

The enrollment of the UAM Band plummeted in 1976–77 as shown in the above photo. Drum major for the school year was JoAnn McCollum with Billy Majors serving as feature twirler. Participation in the group rebounded the following year under the direction of David Koskowski, and new uniforms and a flag line added to a fresh new look when the band took the field. Below the 1977–78 UAM Band poses in concert dress and is shown marching through the streets of Monticello on parade. Director Koskowski is in the dark jacket to the left in the Concert Band photo below.

In the above left photo drum major Lewis Hinkle directs the 1978–79 Weevil Band in the home stands as flag line members end a halftime show with a flourish. In 1979–80 jazz returned to the UAM campus when Dr. Thomas Husak formed the Jazz-Rock Ensemble that played concerts in high schools all over south Arkansas and performed a thirty-minute program on AETN. Also shown below are the Marching Weevil Band and majorettes for 1979–80.

Members of the 1980–81 Weevil Marching Band perform a halftime show on the home campus football field above left, while the Jazz-Rock Ensemble gets in some licks at halftime of a basketball game in the UAM Field House above right. Below, musicians of the 1981–82 UAM Band gather for a group photo, though there were not enough members enrolled to field a marching unit that year; however, they did play for football pep rallies and basketball games. Band director David Koskowski is also shown leading the basketball Pep Band later in the school year.

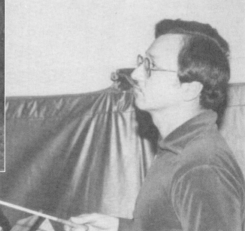

   The 1982–83 UAM school year began with a new band director, Ray Vardeman, a graduate of Ouachita Baptist College, and an increase in band enrollment from twenty-something to forty-one, enabling the campus to field a marching band once again. Beginning a new tradition of high school band marching competition on the UAM campus, the Weevil Marching Band hosted a successful "Battle of the Bands" contest in November staged in the Cotton Boll Stadium. The UAM Band displays its return to the football field and its concert posture in photos above. Though not directly related to the UAM Band, a landmark on the campus since its beginning disappeared in 1983. The "Big Oak," touted as the largest and oldest cherry bark oak tree in Arkansas, was cut down in September 1983, a victim of age and disease. Below are photos of "Big Oak" in its prime and after it was cut down. Also shown is the 1983–84 UAM Concert Band in performance.

The UAM Band's enrollment regained ground with each year Ray Vardaman was the band director. The group was able to perform more intricate football halftime shows, classier basketball game entertainment, and more polished concert performances. A lot of that improvement came as a result of more scholarship monies being made available for Vardaman to attract more talented musicians to the campus. The sixty-three-member UAM Marching Boll Weevils and Concert Band for 1984–85 are shown above along with director Vardaman. Below is the 1985–86 UAM marching unit that fielded sixty-nine musicians. Both years saw Stanford Lewis serving as drum major/field commander.

The 1986–87 UAM Band's Kappa Kappa Psi service fraternity and Tau Beta Sigma service sorority chapters are shown above along with members of that year's Marching Boll Weevil Band on the field in Cotton Boll Stadium. For the following 1987–88 school year, Dr. Kirk Weller (*below center*) was named the new Director of Bands at UAM and the band acquired the new field uniforms pictured below left. Also seen below is the Concert Band performing a spring concert in the Fine Arts Center.

Dr. Kirk Weller

Trumpeter Jim Towers, feature twirler Lana Brian, and flag line member Chris Hendrix were only three of the seventy musicians who made up the UAM Marching Boll Weevil Band for 1988–89. Dubbing itself the "Pride of Southeast Arkansas," the band marched at all home football games, select away games, and both the Drew County Fair Parade and the Warren Christmas Parade.

Gary Meggs, a former alto saxophone player in the Air Force Jazz Band, signed on as the new UAM band director for the 1989–90 school year, though he moved on after only one year in the position. He would return to the job a little over a decade later. His drum major for that year was Rodney Block.

It was decided within the UAM Band ranks in the 1987–88 school year to combine the efforts of the men's Kappa Kappa Psi fraternity chapter and the women's Tau Beta Sigma sorority chapter into one cohesive unit under the Kappa Kappa Psi name, reducing the duplicate officer system and paperwork reporting to the national offices. It also afforded the band students opportunities to work together without gender concerns. The above left photo shows Kappa Kappa Psi members for 1990–91 and the upper right photo features that year's UAM Jazz Band. Below is the 1991–92 UAM Concert Band led by the group's new director, Marty Reynolds, who joined the faculty in 1990. Besides performing at the usual UAM football and basketball games that year, the UAM Band hosted the Arkansas All-State Music Conference and the school's annual high school marching contest on the Monticello campus.

As did the Marching Boll Weevil Band, the UAM basketball Pep Band took its job seriously during the 1992–93 school year. The Pep Band is shown above along with members of UAM's Kappa Kappa Psi service fraternity chapter for the year.

Director Marty Reynolds is shown below left along with some of the nearly one hundred members of the 1993–94 Marching Band living up to their nickname—"The Pride of Southeast Arkansas." Drum major for the year again was Rodney Block.

For 1994–95 Marty Reynolds directed the Boll Weevil Marching Band during the fall term and both the Symphonic and Concert Bands during the spring semester. The Symphonic Band was made up of members who auditioned for a position in the group and played more challenging works for performances on campus as well as for the American School Band Directors Association Convention. Below is a photo taken of members of the 1995–96 Marching Boll Weevil Band on the field during a football halftime show. Also shown is the school's Kappa Kappa Psi chapter for the year.

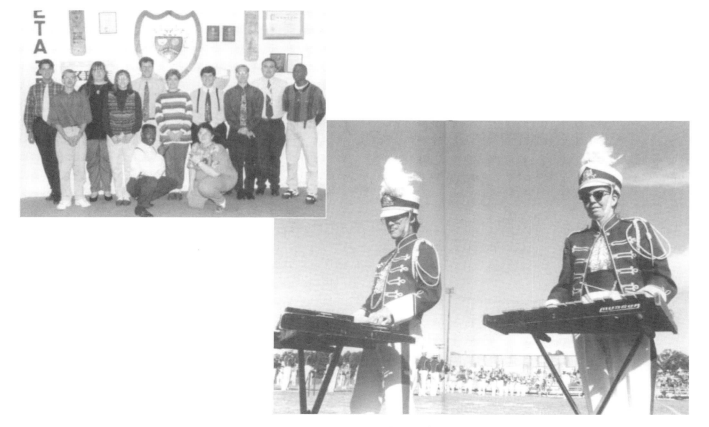

Scott Adkins led "The Pride of Southeast Arkansas" on the field for 1996–97 helping the school's cheerleaders spread that "Weevil Spirit" during parades, football games, pep rallies, and pregame bonfires. Shown above are brass players Chris Floyd and Thomas Wilson and majorette Tiffany Holmes doing their part for the cause. The UAM Band acquired a new Director of Bands in 1997–98, with Michael Davidson from Centenary College in Shreveport stepping into the newly available position. Davidson is shown below in a studio photo and directing the Concert Band during its Christmas Concert. Also pictured is drum major Heath Rhodes conducting the Marching Weevils during a Parent/Family Appreciation Day performance at the chancellor's house on campus.

Director Davidson and members of the 1998–99 Weevil Band are shown above in scenes from the marching season and graduation 1999.

Homecoming 1999 saw the renaming of the UAM football stadium to include that of the school's famous coach from the 1950s and 1960s, Willis "Convoy" Leslie. Henceforth, the locale was known as Convoy Leslie–Cotton Boll Stadium. That year also saw the first downtown Homecoming Parade for UAM since the cessation of the event after 1980. Depicted below are Tim Mullenax (*right*) and Adam Gleason (*bottom*) of the 1999–2000 Marching Boll Weevils and that season's Symphonic Band posing with director Michael Davidson front row left.

Pictured above are members of the UAM Kappa Kappa Psi service fraternity for 2000–2001 along with shots of that season's Marching Boll Weevils and the UAM Symphonic Band. Below are scenes of the UAM Band from the 2001–02 marching season.

The 2002–03 school year was a big one for the UAM band program. The band welcomed back a former Director of Bands in the enthusiastic and hard-working Gary Meggs and acquired its first new set of uniforms since 1987. The UAM Band enrollment had declined somewhat in the previous years, but with dedication and determination, Meggs got the numbers back over the century mark by 2004 and approaching 140 members by the fall of 2005. Above, Meggs is shown in his yearbook photo from the 2003 *Boll Weevil* along with shots of the marching unit appearing in the 2002 Homecoming Parade and in the stands sporting their new uniforms. Note: the school's intercollegiate athletic program competes in the Division II Gulf South Conference.

Below is drum major Brent Miller directing the 2003–04 UAM Band during a halftime program. Also pictured is the marching unit posing for a group shot in the stands at Convoy Leslie Cotton Boll Stadium.

As pictured above and below, the "Pride of Southeast Arkansas" UAM Marching Band grew in size and quality as the twenty-first century progressed with more students qualifying for scholarships. The concert and jazz bands also expanded with two concert and three jazz groups contributing to the music calendar and director Gary Meggs welcoming assistants Les Pack and Bankie Holley in directing the bands. The photos above are from the 2004–05 academic year, and the ones below are from the final football game of the fall 2005 season. Drum major Justin Anders is shown directing the Fighting Weevil Band.

UAM students of instrumental music beginning the fall term of 2006 could choose degree offerings of a Bachelor of Arts in Music and/or a Bachelor of Music Education.

Chapter Eight

The Most Exciting Band in Tiger Land

Ouachita Baptist University
Ouachita Baptist College
Ouachita College

In the mid-1800s there was interest within the Baptist denomination in Arkansas to create an institution of higher learning with roots in the church being that there was none at the time. In fact, there were no state-supported colleges or universities within Arkansas's borders, only a few small floundering church-supported schools of other faiths. By 1851 there were Baptist colleges in most of the other southern states. According to Michael Arrington, the author of *Ouachita Baptist University: The First 100 Years,* Arkansas Baptists, "being a frontier people, moved more slowly than Baptists in the other southern states in recognizing the need for church-related colleges."

After the state's Baptist churches finally organized into the Arkansas Baptist State Convention in September 1848, the group eventually developed "a concern for education, especially for an 'educated' ministry" in the later 1850s. Had the ABSC been able to build on that momentum, there might have been a Baptist college started at that time, but the Civil War intervened and nothing else happened until six schools opened on the associational level in the 1870s, including the Arkadelphia Baptist High School by the Red River Association in 1876. By 1886 only Buckner College at Witcherville and Arkadelphia Baptist High School were still open of those original six due to lack of resources and funding.

It was becoming clear in the early 1880s that it would be advantageous to consolidate the associational schools into one state Baptist institution. Again, according to Arrington, "In 1883 the Convention, fearing lest it 'lag behind the tide of enlightenment,' named a five-man Educational Commission to 'consider the advisability of establishing a Baptist State College, and if thought advisable, to take steps at once to found and fully organize such an institution of learning.'" In 1885 after much discussion and disagreement, a board of trustees was set up to have absolute control of the college and given the authority to build it. The trustees met in Little Rock on April 8, 1886, and heard proposals from eight Arkansas localities on where the college should be built. Then, the following day, on the seventy-second ballot, Arkadelphia was chosen as the site, and a couple of months later, the board of trustees chose John W. Conger, a pastor in Prescott, as the first president of the school. On September 6, 1886, Ouachita College officially opened its doors to 166 students in three departments—primary, secondary, and collegiate. The college began in a large single wood-framed structure near Arkadelphia Baptist High School that had been left empty when the Arkansas School for the Blind moved from the town to Little Rock. Note that the school was originally named Ouachita College; it was not until the Arkansas Baptist State Convention took a significant financial obligation to help support the college in the early 1950s that the word "Baptist" was incorporated into the institution's name—hence, Ouachita Baptist College.

BAND

As for a marching or college band at Ouachita, its existence paralleled that which occurred on many American campuses in the late nineteenth and early twentieth centuries. In the early years of the school a Military Department was established on the campus with leadership and instruction from former Confederate officers. In 1896, the U.S. War Department, the precursor to the modern-day Defense Department, decided that it would contract with a number of college campuses across the country "who could from training and education be depended upon to organize, train, and officer the volunteer forces" of the military. In 1896 Ouachita College officials sought and obtained the opportunity to have such a Military Department on the campus with military officers on the school's staff drilling the enrolled uniformed male students on a regular basis. The photos on the previous page and at the top of this page are from the 1909 OC yearbook and illustrate the Corps Band drilling with the other cadets in front of the Old Main building on the campus and a group shot of the band in a pose taken for that year's *Ouachitonian* (previous to 1909 the yearbook was called the *Bear*). Also included within the yearbook's pages was a copy of the school's copyrighted alma mater, "O-U-A-C-H-I-T-A" and a photo of a Cadet Corps bugler identified simply as Rankin (*shown below*).

Rankin, the Bugler

Ouachita College also had on its campus in 1909–10 an orchestra directed by Mrs. Leora Pryce Miller (*shown above right*), which included female students unlike the Cadet Band that year (*above left*). The "Ouachita March" shown below, written by OC faculty member J. William Taylor, was attached as an addendum to the 1910 yearbook.

With regard to the OC Cadet Band in 1910–11, the yearbook noted about the Military Department's annual pass-in-review parade the following: "We have to doff our hats to the band for their rendition of martial music, for they stirred that patriotism in our breasts that causes men to do their best." Also, a photo of the year's commissioned officers included the band's drum major listed as being Cadet Phil Rankin (*fifth from left*). A cadet was typically in charge of the band rather than a faculty officer. The photos below show the 1911–12 band with the other cadets in drill formation on the campus in front of Old Main and in a group shot.

Adding to the instrumental offerings on the Ouachita campus in 1912–13 was the Philo Ragtime Band shown above left. Since there were no instruments in common between it and the Cadet Band shown at right save for the drums, it is doubtful that any OC students played in both groups. Below is the 1913–14 Ouachita Cadet Band consisting of only brass and percussion instruments.

The 1914–15 Ouachita Cadet Band is shown in the above photo dressed in their traditional white trousers as opposed to the traditional dark pants the other cadets in the battalion wore. No photos exist from the 1916 through the 1923 *Ouachitonian* yearbooks for the cadet military band, though it was mentioned in Arrington's history of the school that a student military program did exist on the campus. Some attrition may have occurred from the school and band due to male student enlistment in the military during World War I, but Ouachita was chosen as a site for the Students' Army Training Corps (SATC) in 1918, which resulted in a rebound in enrollment. At the end of the war the next year the SATC program was converted to the Reserve Officers' Training Corps (ROTC) continuing on into the present. The Ouachita College Orchestra for 1917–18 is shown below.

The Hermisian Orchestra in 1919–20 (*above*) was an adjunct to the Ouachita on-campus Hermisian Literary Society, a men's social organization. Though the music makers played both classical and jazz music, the jazz numbers proved to be more favorably received. By the 1922–23 school year another group of students calling themselves "McCauley and His Serenaders" entered the OC music scene and, from the looks of the yearbook photo below, they enjoyed their merry music-making.

The Ouachita College Military Department's band returned to the yearbook's pages in 1924 (*above left*) and 1925 (*above right*) with these photos of the ROTC Band for those years. The school's orchestra is shown in the photo below for 1925 directed by Wayne McCauley, the young trombone player for whom the jazz band was named on the previous page. He is standing second from left in the back row below. In the 1926 *Ouachitonian*, McCauley was listed in the faculty section as the school's "Director of Band; Bookkeeper."

The photographic record of the 1926–27 Ouachita ROTC Band is shown above left, while the one for 1928–29 is positioned above right. Also shown below is the OC Orchestra for 1928–29 posed on the stage of the campus auditorium. The group was under the direction of the college's noted violin teacher, Professor William Deusinger, standing to the left in the back row.

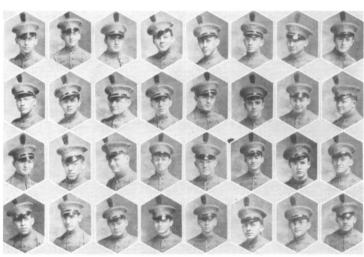

The 1929–30 Ouachita ROTC Band is shown above left in formation on the campus lawn, while the 1931 *Ouachitonian* displayed the group in a similar pose above right. The latter yearbook mentioned that the band played in all battalion parades and reviews as well as performing at athletic contests and other campus functions. Directed by Colonel Fred D. Martin (refer to the preface for additional information about Martin), the group also competed in a military band competition in Biloxi, Mississippi, and performed at the 1931 Old Soldiers Reunion in Montgomery, Alabama. By the 1933–34 school year, Professor William Deusinger was directing both the campus orchestra and the ROTC Band. Below is pictured the 1933–34 OC Band with Deusinger's photo positioned between those of his student director, Roger Dollarhide (*left*), and drum major, Alger Lee Merrill Jr. At lower right are individual photos of the band members that year. Note that the students are wearing new uniforms with plumes in their hats.

In the 1935–36 school year the Ouachita Band was still first and foremost the ROTC Military Band for the campus. But every attempt was made to make the group available for athletic events, parades, and other campus activities. The orchestra, also called "Little Symphony" at the time, allowed women to participate in instrumental music, and the entire instrumental program at the college was overseen by Professor William Deusinger. Above is a portion of the 1936–37 ROTC Band led by student director First Lieutenant Thomas Lavin (*bottom row center*). By 1937–38 Professor William A. Hoppe (*seen below standing to the right in the back row*) was the new director of Ouachita's band program. The drum major was Gene Carroll (*standing center back row*).

A group that performed with the 1937–38 OC Band at football games was the Girl's Pep Squad shown above in a posed shot and one taken during a halftime show with the band off to the left. The squad was sponsored by the band's director, Professor William A. Hoppe. At the end of the 1930s another band joined the Ouachita music scene with the evolution of the "Popular Orchestra." The 1938–39 edition of that group is shown below, directed by student trombonist, James Powers. That year's ROTC Band led by drum major Gene Carroll is also pictured.

New to the band in 1939–40 was director Usher Abel, who led not only the Symphonic Orchestra and the Symphonic Band, but also the ROTC Band when it marched at football games. Shown above are the year's Symphonic and ROTC Bands. Below is the 1940–41 ROTC Band in pass-in-review mode and performing on the football field during a half-time show. Note the difference in uniforms worn for the events. Jimmie Beals was drum major for the year for both the Marching and ROTC Bands and Sergeant Martin Burns was student music director for the ROTC appearances.

Usher Abel, *Director*

In spite of or maybe because of the facts that Ouachita College was not a state-supported school, or that the Great Depression of the 1930s hit the school particularly hard, or that World War II leveled the playing field for all Arkansas colleges, Ouachita's band program seldom had much of an enrollment above forty prior to the 1950s. In fact, most of the time until then it hovered between twenty and thirty members. That was particularly true during the early to mid-1940s. The 1941–42 ROTC Band is shown above left, and the four twirlers who fronted the 1942–43 OC Band that marched at football games and in area parades are pictured above right. Below is the 1943–44 unit.

After World War II colleges and universities all across the country experienced a deluge of servicemen enrolling on their campuses due to the benefits derived from the GI Bill. Ouachita was no exception, and the band program at the school grew as a result. By the 1946–47 school year the OC Band had grown to the size shown in the above photo under the direction of Ouachita alumnus, Martin Burns (*shown to the left in the second row*). The band's majorettes for the year were Martha Jean Carver, Gloria Carpenter, Belle Shyrock, and Mary Alice Linder. The 1948–49 Ouachita Concert Band and director Martin Burns are shown below. Bob Dodson served as drum major for both years shown on this page.

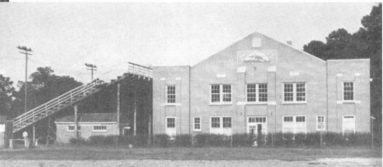

The photo below right above shows the venues where the OC Band supported the football and basketball teams in 1948–49—the football stadium bleachers and field house are back to back. Also shown is the band marching at a game that fall and the band's front line in a pose led by drum major Bobby Smith in front of the campus's legendary tiger mascot sculpture. Another change of directors occurred that year with another Ouachita alumnus, William C. Martin (*below right*), being handed the baton. In uniforms that were purchased prior to the 1947 marching season, the 1949–50 Ouachita Band sits for a concert arrangement alongside a shot of Mitchell Hall, the school's conservatory and scene of the campus's concerts.

The two photos above show the two sides of the 1950–51 Ouachita Band—the Marching and Concert Band in the upper left and the ROTC Band in the lower right. Bill Staggs was the groups' drum major. In yet another turnover in the faculty position of Director of Bands, Ouachita hired John L. Bartlow (*below left*) to helm the campus bands in 1951. He had earned a Master's in Music Education from the University of Kentucky. The 1951–52 marching unit of the Ouachita Band is shown below posing on the floor of the campus field house with drum major Leroy Summers front and center. Note that the college officially added the word "Baptist" to its name in the early 1950s to read Ouachita Baptist College when the Arkansas Baptist State Convention significantly increased its financial support to the school.

The fall of 1952 saw still another new band director for the Ouachita Band in Harry A. Putt (*above, beside a photo of the 1952–53 OBC Band*), who had his Master's in Music from Cincinnati Conservatory; and then Herbert Cecil (*below, next to a concert setting of the 1954–55 OC Band*) came on board in the fall of 1954 with his Ph.D. from the University of Rochester. The Ouachita Band (*below right*) is shown marching through the streets of Arkadelphia during Homecoming 1954.

Above is the 1955–56 Ouachita Tiger Band outfitted from top to toe in brand-new uniforms for the fall football season. And below is the OBC Band in rehearsal with its new director for the 1956–57 school year. He was Florida State doctoral recipient, James T. Luck, who would direct the band for a year and then hand the reins over to the legendary W. Francis McBeth while retaining the direction of the Little Symphony.

The two photos above highlight the 1957–58 Ouachita Band both in a concert setting on the campus's auditorium stage and in marching formation during that fall's Homecoming Parade through downtown Arkadelphia. The president of the band for the school year was Ann Seward, first chair clarinetist. For 1958–59 the band (*below*) supported the football team throughout the fall season as well as performed regular concert performances on the campus. Wordy Buckner (first chair clarinetist) served as drum major.

The effectiveness of W. Francis McBeth's direction was evident in the growth of the Ouachita Band during his tenure with the group, growing to fifty-eight members by 1959–60. McBeth's arrangement of existing melodies and composition of original pieces was becoming known by that time, and his reputation was gaining ground. He is even credited with arranging the music for the Tiger fight song. Student director Wordy Buckner is shown above taking the band through its paces. Below, the 1960–61 OBC Band is shown playing for invited high school students in the school's auditorium on Tiger Day and parading down Main Street during Homecoming 1960.

For the 1961–62 school year the above five women made up the Ouachita majorette line, who were joined in front of the band by drum major Ellis Melton. That year the Jazz Band (*above right*) entertained at various school functions. Though remaining on the faculty of the college's Music Department, Francis McBeth yielded the baton to Marvin Lawson (*pictured below*) as the new Director of Bands in 1962–63, with Lawson holding that position for the next twenty-two years. Shown below are the Ouachita Choir and Band as they performed at the 1963 Arkansas Baptist State Convention in Little Rock under the direction of Dr. James Luck.

The 1963–64 Ouachita Marching Tigers are shown above on the field in a combined show with the Henderson Band during the inter-city Thanksgiving football classic. The Tiger Band is also pictured on parade during Homecoming festivities of 1963, led by drum major Ellis Melton. In addition, the band gave three formal concerts on-campus, played regularly at Chapel, and made a three-day tour of central Arkansas high schools. The 1964–65 edition of the Ouachita Band numbered sixty members and is shown below during an indoor rehearsal on campus. The twirlers in the band's front line are also featured below right. Proudly for the school, it attained university status on January 14, 1965, officially changing its name to Ouachita Baptist University.

By the fall of 1965, the Ouachita Band had grown to the point that it had run out of uniforms, and percussion players and some other musicians had to be fitted in poplin jackets close in color to the regular band jackets. The above photos show the band attired as such. For the 1965 and 1966 marching seasons Doyle Combs served as drum major. Ready to begin the fall of 1966, the band received the new uniforms worn below by the percussion section of the 116 member marching unit for halftime shows and parades and by the record 103-piece Concert Band for formal concerts. Additionally, the Jazz Band was judged as one of the top ten in the nation and appeared in the finals contest at Notre Dame University.

By the school year 1967–68, not only were the Marching and Concert Bands gaining notoriety under Marvin Lawson's direction and an occasional premier work by Francis McBeth, smaller instrumental groups at OBU were also presenting performances such as the Woodwind Quintet and the Brass Choir shown above. Though the membership rolls of the 1968–69 Ouachita Bands were down somewhat, the band continued its full calendar of events including a spring tour of Arkansas high schools. Below are Marvin Lawson and that year's Concert Band. Steve Hand and David Glaze served as the marching band's drum majors for the fall of both 1967 and 1968. In the mid-1960s, OBU adopted a peppy arrangement of the hymn favorite, "Will the Circle Be Unbroken," as the school's fight song, which is still used as of this printing.

The photos above show the 1969–70 Ouachita Brass Ensemble and students rehearsing for campus concerts played in OBU's Mitchell Hall in the winter and outdoors in the spring. Assisting Marvin Lawson that year in directing the eighty-member Marching Tigers and sixty-member Concert Band was graduate assistant Ray Vardaman. For the 1970–71 school year the majorettes below performed twirling exhibitions during halftime shows and parades, including newly elected governor Dale Bumpers's inaugural parade held in January in Little Rock.

David Henderson was drum major and president of the 1971–72 Ouachita Bands shown above in the stands during a home game and on the stage of Mitchell Hall. Francis McBeth received his honorary doctorate from Hardin Simmons University, won one of his many ASCAP awards, and became the permanent conductor of the Arkansas Symphony Orchestra in 1971. Below is the 1972–73 OBU Band marching in the 1972 Homecoming Parade and Lucious Postell practicing on his horn outdoors.

The 1974 *Ouachitonian* yearbook states that there were ninety-six members of the OBU Marching Band in the fall of 1973 and seventy-seven students in the Concert Band (*shown above*). The photos below present a focused 1974–75 Ouachita Band on the field making some serious and yet fun music. Also pictured is the OBU majorette lineup that season.

As a result of a large grant from the Mabee Foundation of Tulsa and matching funds from Arkansas Baptist churches, OBU was able to construct a new Fine Arts Center on the campus named after the foundation, which was moved into in February 1975 and dedicated that fall. At the dedication, the OBU Band played "Ouachita Fanfare" written by the campus's composer-in-residence, Dr. Francis McBeth. Photos above are of the 1975–76 band, and those below are of the 1976–77 band. David Chism assisted director Marvin Lawson with the band program, and Taylor Brown was the group's drum major.

OBU Stage Band provides back-up music for Bob Hope performance.

For the 1977–78 school year the OBU Band donned the new uniforms shown above that were ordered the previous spring; it was the first new wardrobe for the group in eleven years. A notable event for the OBU Stage Band was an appearance won by the musicians in a collegiate talent contest held to perform with entertainer Bob Hope in an October show in Pine Bluff. The Stage Band performed as an opening act and as backup band during the show. Choir Day on the OBU campus was traditionally where Baptist churches from all over the state sent choir members to perform during the second home football game each year with the OBU Band accompanying. In the fall of 1978 for the first time, those who played instruments from the churches were allowed to play with the OBU Band during the performance. The 1978–79 OBU Band is shown below.

Calling themselves the "Showcase of Ouachita," band members began marching with more contemporary corps-style methods, leaving the military cadences behind. Director Lawson was quoted in the 1980 *Ouachitonian* yearbook as saying, "Our music will lean toward more pop, jazz and classical styles. There will be no more marching music." A new flag line was also added to the band's ranks in the fall of 1979. The new uniforms received the previous year also included a warmer weather component seen above. The flag and majorette lines for the 1980–81 season are shown below.

The 1981–82 OBU Pep Band (*above*), directed by Marvin Lawson, performed at pep rallies on the school campus and also traveled to away games to support the football team. Additionally shown above are the Marching Tigers performing during a halftime show and Rita Sutterfield directing the band in her third season as the group's drum major. In February 1982, the Concert Band was invited to appear at the annual Arkansas Music Educators Convention in Pine Bluff. Below are scenes from the 1982–83 OBU Band's marching season.

In what was Marvin Lawson's last year as Director of Bands at OBU, 1983–84 turned out to be as full of activities as any other in his twenty-two-year tenure atop the podium. Numbering almost one hundred members enrolled, the Marching Band performed at football games, the Pep Band traveled to out-of-town games and played at pep rallies, and the Concert Band performed a number of concerts both outdoors and in the recital hall on campus. Lawson (*above right*) is pointing out needed adjustments during rehearsal for the "Showcase of Ouachita." Starting in the fall of 1984 Craig Hamilton took over as the new OBU Band director. The group was noticeably down in membership to about fifty musicians, but the performances continued nonetheless.

For 1985–86 the enrollment figures were up from the year before and director Hamilton helped to establish chapters of the Kappa Kappa Psi band fraternity and Tau Beta Sigma band sorority on the OBU campus. Hamilton also pushed more up-tempo jazz and contemporary music into all aspects of the band repertoire. Members of the Marching Tigers that fall are shown above going through their halftime paces, while the Jazz Band rehearses for a gig. Drum major Rod Mays for 1986–87 below led the OBU Band on the field and on parade in newly received uniforms for the fall term.

The above photo reflects the 1987–88 OBU Band's support of the football team from the home stands. The photo at right is Jazz Band trumpeter Mark Roberts playing for an on-campus jazz concert. During the year, the Jazz Band hosted the campus's first-ever Jazz Festival in the Mabee Fine Arts recital hall with several jazz bands from around the state participating. Also that year the Concert Band grew to sixty-three members. Concert Band musicians for 1988–89 below are shown performing at the Baptist Convention missionary commissioning service. Below left is majorette Paige Umholtz during halftime rehearsal.

Beth Anne Rankin (*above left*) was OBU's feature twirler for three years beginning in the fall of 1989, the first since 1984. That spring, the school's Concert Band traveled to Columbus, Ohio, to perform at a conference for the Christian Instrumental Directors Association (CIDA). Above right, a Marching Tiger concentrates on his music during Homecoming 1989, while above center band members bow their heads for the invocation prior to the kick-off for Homecoming 1990. Below, percussionists for the 1991 edition of the "Showcase of Ouachita" eye drum major Kim Madlock for a halftime tempo, and Craig Hamilton conducts the Concert Band during a concert on campus.

Under Craig Hamilton's direction, the 1992–93 OBU Marching Tigers continued to grow in numbers and perfect their football halftime shows as shown above. A smaller Pep Band also ignited the fans at on-campus basketball games. Another segment of the band program, the Jazz Band under Barry McVinney's tutelage (*above right*), continued to excel that year. A relatively new trombone ensemble for OBU, the Ouachibones directed by Dr. Sim Flora, attracted some positive attention for the school during the 1993–94 school year with weekend run-outs to area churches and schools. A few of those players are shown below during a halftime performance in Little Rock's War Memorial Stadium led by drum major Christi Watts. Also pictured are that season's color guard and majorette line.

For 1994–95 Dr. Craig Hamilton (he received his Ph.D. from the University of North Texas in 1994) added a new instrumental group to the OBU curriculum with the Wind Ensemble composed of the top band members who performed in the newly completed Jones Performing Arts Center and toured throughout the year. That season's Marching Tigers, led by drum major Mac McMurry above, were ninety-eight in number, the largest enrollment since the 1970s. Dr. W. Francis McBeth, composer-in-residence at OBU (*pictured below*), retired from the school at the end of the 1995–96 school year. To celebrate his thirty-nine years of service to OBU, the School of Fine Arts presented a two-evening salute to him with the band and choir performing a number of his works, and the recital hall in Mabee Fine Arts Center was named in his honor. Also shown below are the Concert Band in performance and Kristi Cannon twirling with the 1995–96 Marching Tiger Band.

A big thrill for many members of the OBU Band in 1996 was the trip to Hawaii to play for the Missionary Kids Conference. Seventy students and fourteen faculty and staff went to Honolulu and, after practicing during the afternoons (*shown above left*), played for the evening programs, accompanying special guests and artists and playing sacred music with the choir. Also shown above center is drum major Cari Martin directing the OBU band (*right*) during a halftime show in the fall of 1996. Below left, Dr. Craig Hamilton discusses a marching rehearsal with some of his students in 1997 going over points about the show and music. At right are three of the band's majorettes for that fall performing during a halftime show. It is worth noting that the devastating tornado that hit Arkadelphia on March 1, 1997, left OBU with relatively minor physical damage.

In the fall of 1998 OBU Band members were able to complete their new uniform outfits above with the purchase of jackets and hats to go with the new trousers that had been ordered and worn with windbreakers the previous year. The new white, purple, and gold wardrobe got a real workout at home games played at A. U. Williams Field and in area parades and marching contests in Jesseville and War Memorial Stadium. On June 1, 1999, two OBU members of the Ouachita Singers were among a number of people killed in an American Airlines plane crash at Little Rock's National Airport. Arkadelphia and OBU mourned their deaths, and eventually through faith and courage, moved on with their lives. Photos below show 1999–2000 OBU Band members doing just that.

For the 110-member 2000–2001 OBU Marching Tigers the two biggest games during which they were able to perform were the traditional first game rivalry with "across the ravine" Henderson State University and the subsequent "alumni-en-masse" Homecoming battle. Above is that season's band performing a halftime show consisting of *La Suerte de los Tontos*, *Pegasus*, and *Echano*. Also above are Kappa Kappa Psi band fraternity members playing for an on-campus Christmas party. The year 2001–02 saw Dr. Craig Hamilton yield the athletic band director duties to Matt Fredrickson, while retaining the title of Director of Bands along with conducting the Wind Ensemble. The year's lone majorette to twirl with the band was Jenna Mazoch, shown below center. Drum major was Tiffany Key.

In the fall of 2002 the OBU campus found itself with its second director of athletic bands in two years. He was Robert Hesse, the highly respected band director from Arkadelphia High School (*shown in the photo above right*). With one hundred members in its ranks the band experienced a new direction with Hesse, "known for his innovation and exciting marching bands" (quoting Dr. Craig Hamilton from the 2003 *Quachitonian*, Director of Bands at OBU). Below the 2003–04 Marching Tiger Band—"The Most Exciting Band in Tiger Land"—with drum major Lindsey Barber is shown during a half-time show featuring a contemporary drill formation with its ninety-four-member unit. Also popular during the school year was Tiger Jam, the pep band that played at basketball games, and Tiger Blast performances at the Tiger Tunes events.

Holding the Form: *The Most Exciting Band in Tiger Land performs at halftime. Band members rehearsed about seven hours a week to prepare for their performances. Photo By Jessica McFadden*

    With its ranks numbering over one hundred students (impressive where the entire student body numbers only about fifteen hundred), the 2004–05 school year began with Lindsey Barber once again leading the OBU Band onto the A. W. Williams home football field as its field commander (drum major). By the 2005 fall football season, during which the team competed in the Division II Gulf South Conference, 115 band members were part of the "Most Exciting Band in Tiger Land" matching the size the band had been at its peak in the mid-1960s. The band's drum major that season was Sarah Beene. As of this writing, Robert Hesse (*below right*) remains as the enthusiastic director of the outdoor OBU Marching Band and the innovative indoor marching unit called "Tiger Blast," which stages very popular performances each semester in the campus auditorium. Dr. Craig Hamilton remains as director of the forty-member Wind Ensemble and twenty-member Jazz Band. Those two men show what faith and talent can do for a private university band program.

    As this book went to press, coursework leading to an undergraduate degree on the OBU campus pertaining to instrumental studies included a Bachelor of Music in Performance, a Bachelor of Arts with Music Emphasis, and a Bachelor of Music Education.

Chapter Nine

Thundering Herd

Harding University
Harding College
Arkansas Christian College/Harper College

Harding University had its beginnings not in the town of Searcy where it is currently located, but in the towns of Harper, Kansas, and Morrilton, Arkansas, and at the two junior colleges in those communities. Harper College in Harper, Kansas, was a junior college with its roots in the Church of Christ faith founded in 1915 with about fifty students. Three years later, a sister school, Cordell Christian College in Cordell, Oklahoma, closed, and a number of its faculty members joined the Harper College staff, including J. N. Armstrong and his wife, Woodson Harding Armstrong, and L. C. Sears. The following year Mr. Armstrong became the president of Harper College and led the school to an enrollment of about three hundred students by the fall of 1923.

The second junior college to provide a limb to Harding's family tree was Arkansas Christian College in Morrilton, Arkansas, also a Church of Christ school; it was founded by Mr. and Mrs. Gus Hill of Conway in 1919. Mrs. Hill had encouraged the denomination's state churches to support such a school, and Morrilton came up with the best bid for the proposed school, including forty acres, $70,000 in cash, and free utilities for four years. Classes began there in 1922 with Harvard graduate A. S. Croom as president, even though construction of the school's buildings was not completed.

By 1924 both of the above junior colleges were in trouble. Harper College was in dire financial straits mainly due to Armstrong's lack of business acumen, and Arkansas Christian College had few students and faculty on board due to Croom's concentration on the building program and not on recruitment. Croom became aware of Harper College's financial problems and proposed to Armstrong (with the full approval of the Arkansas Christian College board) that the two schools should merge. With Morrilton offering another $24,000 to pay off Harper's debts, most of the Harper faculty moved to Arkansas.

The following paragraphs are from Jason Jewell's master's thesis about the history of the Department of Music at Harding University:

> Morrilton was without a doubt a better location than Harper for a school affiliated with Churches of Christ. The religious group was, and still is, strongest in the region of the country known as "the Bible Belt," of which Arkansas is a part. Over 25,000 residents of the state claimed affiliation, a statistic which boded well for enrollment and support. In 1924 Morrilton had about 5000 inhabitants, four miles of paved roads, four banks, and a Carnegie Library. It was located in the southern foothills of the Ozarks, which Harding's catalog described as "one of the most beautiful, fertile, and healthful sections of the state."

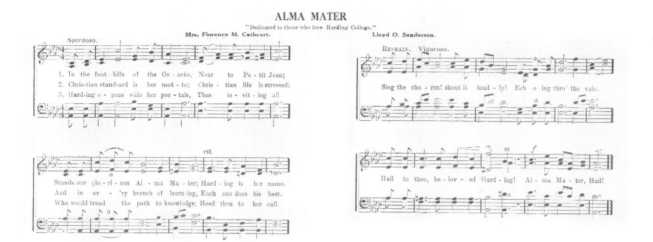

The combination of faculty and assets from the two junior colleges enabled the newly consolidated institution to become a standard four-year college. The Arkansas State Board of Education granted official recognition on June 4, 1926. The newly formed board of trustees, which was basically the same as Arkansas Christian's, chose the name Harding College to honor the memory of James A. Harding, a prominent preacher among Churches of Christ who had died in 1922. J. N. Armstrong was named president, A. S. Croom vice-president, and L. C. Sears dean of the college. The college was divided into a College of Arts and Sciences with 14 faculty and a School of Fine Arts with five faculty. Enrollment for the 1924–1925 school year was a mere 77 students; another 200 were enrolled in the Harding elementary and high schools . . .

At this time music was a subdivision of the School of Fine Arts, a relatively modest extension of the college which also included art and expression (drama). Within the School of Fine Arts were 'departments' of piano, violin, and vocal music, each of which normally had only one faculty member, often not even a full-time one. The school was not qualified to offer degrees in any area; participating students worked toward a diploma or certificate, usually at the same time they were pursuing a Bachelor of Arts degree in the College of Arts and Sciences.

In the early years of the school the turnover rate of the music faculty left few teachers remaining on the staff more than three or four years. Although there were some instrumental classes offered in violin and piano, the most prevalent music courses taken were those in voice and choir since they didn't require the purchase of expensive musical instruments.

Both intercollegiate football and a college orchestra were introduced to the Harding campus at the school's formation in 1924. The team played only four games before their coach was killed in a car accident, but their record included wins over College of the Ozarks and Hendrix. The orchestra was begun with virtually all beginners under the direction of faculty member Fannie Marie Moody pictured above with the school's 1924–25 initial group.

In the fall of 1925 the orchestra was under the direction of a faculty member by the name of Professor Orr, seen above to the extreme right in the top photo. By the summer term of 1926, the Harding College Orchestra had made a five-week tour across the state of Arkansas and parts of Missouri performing community concerts. The second photo above is from the 1928 *Petit Jean* yearbook showing the orchestra under the direction of Iven H. Hensley (*standing at right*). His wife also played violin in the group and was instructor of violin at the college for a period of time.

Although a Professor A. De Chaudron was listed in the 1929 Harding yearbook as director of the orchestra, I. H. Hensley was once again mentioned as director of the unit in the 1933 *Petit Jean* as pictured above. Hensley also taught education and psychology.

By 1934 with enrollment up to three hundred students, the Morrilton campus buildings were bursting at their seams regarding classroom and dormitory space. Two years earlier the financially strapped Methodists in Arkansas had to close Galloway College in Searcy, an all-female school, which attracted the attention of President Armstrong and others in the Harding community. Eventually, the sale of the Galloway campus was made to the Harding board of trustees for $75,000, "a bargain considering that the Galloway campus was three time the size of the Morrilton campus and contained more, albeit older, facilities. Following the purchase, the board of trustees disposed of the Morrilton campus and moved Harding College to Searcy in the summer of 1934" (cited from Jewell's thesis). (Author's note: The school's alma mater which was written in 1925 by Florence Cathcart and set to music by Lloyd Sanderson, both members of Harding's faculty, refers to the school's being "In the foothills of the Ozarks, Near to Petit Jean"; because of the move to Searcy, it has since been modified to "Near the foothills of the Ozarks, Midst of hill and plain.")

Robert B. Boyd

After the 1931 fall season, intercollegiate football was discontinued on the Harding campus, but intramural games were still played. Intercollegiate basketball was given a chance up until 1939, though the roundballers did not belong to any conference. To support the intramural football and intercollegiate basketball efforts, a Harding freshman in the fall of 1933 took the initiative and formed what he called the Pep Band among students on campus who had their own access to instruments. His name was Robert Boyd (*shown in the back row at right in the above group photo*).

Robert Boyd was the very popular director of the Harding Pep Band for the four years he attended the college until he completed studies in 1937. Note that no course credit was given to students participating in the band, unlike those enrolled in the orchestra under the direction of Miss Lois Albright shown above in a photo from the 1935 yearbook.

Note that Harding played intercollegiate football from 1924 to 1931, but only played on-campus intramural games between 1932 and 1958; intercollegiate basketball was introduced in 1932. In his thesis, Jason Jewell noted that Boyd was the director of the band for all four years he was at Harding "except for a period of about two months in the fall of 1936 when a Robert Shanks was hired to direct the band and orchestra." Save for the time mentioned above, the orchestra was under the direction of Lois Albright from 1934 to 1938, and she was considered one of the finest musicians ever to teach at the school.

The top photo above shows Robert Boyd (*front row left, next to the drum*) and the other members of the 1936–37 Harding Pep Band. After Boyd graduated in 1937, sophomore Hugh Rhodes led the band for one year (*shown in the second photo above to the right front of the bass drum*). And then faculty chorus director and future Music Department head Leonard Kirk (*shown with baton below*) directed the group during the 1938–39 school year. The 1939 *Petit Jean* yearbook noted in its pages that "the Pep Band has been outstanding at all basketball games and has led the spirit of the cheering section."

By the fall of 1939 senior Claude Guthrie was directing the Harding College Band in performing not only at athletic contests but also at concerts in its own right. Note the larger size of the group above in a photo from the 1940 *Petit Jean* yearbook. Guthrie is standing at back left.

After Guthrie graduated in 1940, sophomore William Laas took over as the college band and orchestra conductor (he is shown with both groups above during the 1940–41 school year). After intercollegiate basketball was discontinued at Harding in 1939, the band soon found itself without a group for which to cheer (save for campus intramural football). They did perform at various campus and community events, but often found themselves duplicating the orchestra's efforts. Eventually, band members who so desired were blended into the existing orchestra. A comment accompanying the photo of the band from the 1941 *Petit Jean* yearbook noted, "the band added sparkle to many events and various instrumental groups within its number—the brass quartet, trumpet trio, woodwind ensemble, and soloists—entertained at special occasions."

William Laas

William Laas remained as conductor of the orchestra at Harding College until he graduated in the spring of 1943 (he is shown above conducting his final concert that year). With as many as forty students in the group at its peak practicing three times a week, the orchestra gave U.S.O. concerts during the war along with usual chapel and assembly programs and lyceum numbers on campus. After a short stay in his native Texas after graduation he returned to Searcy and became the director of the Searcy High School Band, eventually supervising a young man by the name of George Baggett in his semester of student teaching in 1950.

After Laas graduated from Harding in 1943, there is no indication that there was an orchestra on the campus the following year, though there is mention and photos of M. D. Chronic as conductor of the campus orchestra in the 1945 and 1946 yearbooks. The photo above is from the 1946 *Petit Jean* with Chronic holding the baton at left.

There is no indication of a band or orchestra at Harding from the fall of 1946 until 1951. As Jason Jewell stated in his master's thesis, "The absence of a band during this time highlights the relative lack of interest in instrumental music on campus." While there was no band or orchestra present, the Chorus numbered over two hundred and traveled extensively on a healthy budget. The new departmental chair, Erle T. Moore, would change that in 1951 with the goal of having a well-balanced Music Department. He set out not to penalize the Chorus, but to restore and improve the instrumental presence on the campus.

One of the challenges to a band's or orchestra's survival at Harding was the lack of adequate facilities for faculty offices and rehearsal areas. Divided between space in the old Godden Hall and Gray Gables buildings, neither had any soundproofing, thereby hampering rehearsal schedules. And evening practices could not be held in Godden Hall because it also functioned as a dormitory. Being before the time of widespread air-conditioning, temperature extremes also took a toll on students, faculty, and instruments. In 1950, the fifty-two-year-old Godden Hall was razed and a new music building was built on the east side of the campus primarily with recycled materials from Godden Hall. With students assisting in the project, workers carried "wood, brick, and tile across campus" from the previous site where a new administrative building was concurrently being built.

Ironically, the man whom Moore wanted to head the reinstated band program at Harding attended and graduated from Harding during the time that there was no band offered. George E. Baggett, having been very involved in his high school band, attended the school between 1946 and 1950, receiving a degree in music education. But with an offer by Moore to restart the band program after attaining a graduate degree, Baggett later enrolled at Kansas City University, receiving his master's diploma in instrumental music. Beginning in the summer of 1951, Baggett is shown standing at right in the top photo with his first Harding Band and at the rear right in the second photo with the 1952–53 band.

The top photo is of the 1953–54 Harding Band with their first set of uniforms—maroon jackets and gray pants for the men and gray skirts for the women. By the fall of 1954 there were thirty-five college and high school students in the Harding Band. Though there were enough participating students at the College and the Academy to have separate choral groups at both of the schools, that was not yet a fact concerning the band. The second photo is of the 1955–56 Harding Band. The group played at Academy football games, the Band–Academy Chorus Concert, and its own separate concert.

The symphony was revived on the Harding campus in 1955, known as "Symphonette," with Kenneth Davis conducting and George Baggett playing among the students on baritone. In the above photo, Mr. Davis is standing at extreme right.

The photo above shows the Harding Band marching through campus after the Homecoming Parade in 1955. During the school year the band took a big step by going on its first tour, presenting a total of six concerts in east Arkansas and in west Tennessee. Selected band members also participated in the Arkansas Intercollegiate Band for the first time.

In addition to the Harding Band (*shown above in concert formation*), the MOODS appeared on campus and in the pages of the *Petit Jean* yearbook in 1956–57. A polished thirteen-piece swing band under the direction of senior George Oliver, the latter group made its initial appearance on the "Student Association Presents" program, and, according to the yearbook, "found an immediate and enthusiastic welcome."

According to the 1958 and 1959 *Petit Jean* yearbooks the Harding Band not only played for assemblies and Academy ballgames, but the group also marched in parades in Searcy and participated in the White County Fair. In addition the Pep Band added musical spirit to the basketball games, which had been reinstated in intercollegiate play after being halted in 1939. Director Baggett conducts the 1957–58 Harding Band in a concert on campus in the top photo, while the 1958–59 band is featured in the second photo.

In the fall of 1959 after an absence from the campus since 1931, intercollegiate football returned to Harding with full support from students and alumni alike. The team posted a 1–5 season record, but the Bison showed that they were back and ready to compete in the AIC the following year. The 1959–60 Bison Band above poses for the yearbook in the upper photo, while the 1960–61 group does the same in the lower photo.

As can be seen in the top photo of the 1961–62 Harding Bison Band, members are still wearing the same vintage uniforms they received when the group first donned the garments in 1953. The second photo shows the 1962–63 Concert Band in civilian attire. According to Jewell, during the 1950s and 1960s Baggett divided his time "between teaching duties at the college and at Harding Academy, where he taught music classes and directed the chorus from 1953 until 1963. Eventually the demands of teaching at both schools began to tell, and Baggett, with Moore's encouragement, made a request for a full-time teaching assignment at the college, to which President (George) Benson agreed." Because of student-led fundraisers the Bison Band opened the 1963–64 school year with new uniforms, seen in photos below in both marching and concert versions. The group also passed the fifty-member mark for the first time and was led onto the field at halftime by drum major Jerry Bolls.

George Baggett, MA
Assistant Professor
Music

For the fall of 1964 Jerry Bolls was once again drum major for the Bison Band, and Martha Pitner joined the ranks as Harding's first feature twirler as the group provided music and precision drills at the football games. Note the classic "H" formation staged during the playing of the school's alma mater.

Also note the classic yellow-gold overlay that was worn over the concert tuxedo uniform of the 1965–66 Bison Band to give the group a choice of looks.

The above photos illustrate the 1966–67 Bison Band performing drills during the Maryville–Harding game and posed in concert formation. John Bowen served his second of five seasons as drum major that year, while George Baggett was in his sixteenth year as Director of Bands and serving double duty as the Chorale director for a time. After having members selected for the Arkansas Intercollegiate Band over the previous ten years, Harding College was the host to the Thirteenth Annual AIC Band Convention in the spring of 1968 with fourteen Arkansas colleges in attendance. Pictured below is the 1967–68 Bison Band, which added two majorettes to its marching unit during the fall season, and the Pep Band that entertained at basketball games on campus.

In the fall of 1969 the entire Music Department was the beneficiary of a remodeled music building with a generous donation made in memory of a former Harding student. Officially named the Claud Rogers Lee Music Center, it provided modern vocal and instrumental facilities. The 1969–70 Bison Band is pictured above at the dedication. The photos below show the precision of the Bison Marching Band during the 1970 Homecoming Parade and the determination of the band in the stands during a football game. Ken Stewart was drum major for the group during the 1970 and 1971 seasons.

The above photo of Harding's Stage Band for 1971–72 under the student direction of Rick Guyer shows off the group in ties and sport coats as they dressed in performing before area high schools in promotion of the college. Also pictured are snapshots from rehearsals during marching season. The photo below of the Bison Band in the fall of 1972 records the group's marching through downtown Searcy in the White County Fair Parade, led by drum major Steve Burton. The football team finished the season with its best-ever record 10–1 overall and 5–1 AIC for its first AIC title. The team also won its first postseason bowl game, 30–27 against Langston in the Cowboy Bowl played in Lawton, Oklahoma.

As can be seen in the above photo, the Bison Band grew larger for 1973–74 and additional uniforms of the existing style had to be purchased the following year to accommodate an even larger band. Steven Holder, Warren Casey, and Johnny Nash alternated serving as drum majors for the year. In addition to marching at football home games and in the Homecoming Parade, the Heber Springs Christmas Parade, and the White County Fair Parade, the band also presented a series of on-campus concerts during the year and a tour of concerts in nearby states in the spring. The Stage Band was directed by Steve Holder that year. During the 1974–75 school year two Pep Bands were created to play at the basketball games to accommodate the interest in students wanting to perform. The Nash Pep Band is pictured below left, and the Cox Pep Band is pictured below right. During the summer of 1974 Director George Baggett completed his doctorate in music education.

Harding drum majors for the 1975 marching season included Warren Casey and Johnny Nash. Nash served as drum major for four years and Casey three; Casey would also later become the Bison Band director in 1982.

The above three photos are of members of the Bison Band as they appeared in the 1977 *Petit Jean* yearbook. Upper left is Sarah Sewell marching with her flute during a halftime presentation; lower left are members of the trombone section entertaining at a pep rally on campus; and at right is Johnny Nash as the band's lone drum major that year. Note that at the beginning of the 1976–77 school year separate band and orchestra units were established at Harding Academy, thereby making the Harding Bison Band exclusively a collegiate group for the first time in its history. From its inception the Harding Band had been a combination of College and Academy students. And lastly, the John Prock–coached football Bisons again won the AIC title with a 5–1 conference record and 7–5 overall. They later lost their postseason bowl appearance against Abilene Christian in the Shrine Bowl played in Pasadena, Texas.

The Bison Band in the fall of 1977 boasted a record 105 members in addition to a 19-member flag corps. Halftime shows for the year featured music from *Rocky, Star Wars,* and a medley of national food-chain themes. Shown above are sousaphone player Jerry Wolfe and majorettes Susan Willis and Diana Floyd, who fronted the band with drum major Mickey Cox. As it had for eighteen years the Harding College Band began the 1978 fall term with a music camp at Camp Tahkodah near Floral, directed by Dr. George Baggett. That year the band also appeared at the beginning of football games assisted by an honor guard composed of men from the Air National Guard and the Naval and Marine Center. Drum majors Mickey Cox and Mark Hudson led the band through the first season the group had been nicknamed "The Thundering Herd."

The most obvious change on the Harding campus in 1979 was the change of status of the school from a college to a university; henceforth, the campus would be known as Harding University. To symbolize that change during a football halftime show, the Thundering Herd morphed an "HC" formation on the field above left into the "HU" seen above right.

The fall of 1980 saw a drop in enrollment in the Thundering Herd from 110 the previous year to only 80 members in September. However, student director and drum major Mark Hudson was quoted in the 1981 *Petit Jean* yearbook, saying, "This group picked up the new music and marching drills very quickly." Fellow drum major Bill Anthony is shown directing the band in the "H" formation below. The second photo below features student director Joel Ragland conducting the band during the Outdoor Spring Concert.

The 1981–82 school term was the final year that Dr. George Baggett served as director of the Thundering Herd Marching Band and the Concert Band at Harding. Deteriorating visual health resulting in eye surgery necessitated his eventual handing over the reins to someone else. He would remain on the faculty, teaching music courses and private lessons until retiring in 1993. The above photo shows Baggett at extreme right with his last concert/marching band. Drum majors at left were Bill Anthony and Lisa Shoaf. Also pictured is that year's Stage Band. New to the Harding music staff in the fall of 1982 was Warren Casey (*standing at right in the photo below*), a former drum major and member of the Harding Marching, Concert, Stage, and Pep Bands. Though the number of members dropped to fewer than fifty that year, they marched smartly under drum major Lisa Shoaf's lead in their gaucho-styled uniforms introduced the previous year.

The fall of 1983 brought a new feature twirler in Dede Clements and a new drum major in Terry Girdley. The above photo illustrates the Thundering Herd's precision drills marched at halftime at the football games. In the spring the Concert Band toured with concerts performed in Alabama, Georgia, and Florida. The Thundering Herd for 1984–85 (*below*) resembled more a drum and bugle corps than a college band with its heavy emphasis on brass instruments and percussion. As his predecessor had done for many years, Warren Casey started off the school year with a week of preseason preparation at Camp Tahkodah forty miles from Searcy. Richard Kalnins was drum major for the year, and Lisa Reed led the Pep Band. Also shown below is that year's Concert Band.

In addition to directing the Thundering Herd and the Concert Band, Warren Casey was also the director of the Jazz Band, which is pictured above in a photo taken from the 1986 *Petit Jean* yearbook. It should be noted that the Stage Band had been renamed the Jazz Band on Casey's arrival as director in 1982 and attained credit course status that year. During spring break of 1986 the Concert Band presented a series of concerts on a tour through Oklahoma, Kansas, Colorado, and Nebraska. In the photo below left the 1986–87 Thundering Herd is shown sporting new uniforms, which returned the band's look to the more traditional West Point design. Field direction that season was under drum major Laura Baker. Also pictured is that season's Jazz Band, a fixture of the annual campus Spring Sing musical extravaganza since 1974 and still going strong as of this writing.

When the Harding Band took to the field in the fall of 1987, enrollment in the group crept over the fifty-member mark for the first time since Warren Casey had taken over as director in 1982. Shown above in their smart white-jacketed uniforms, the Thundering Herd was led on the field by drum major Felicia Voyles. Also shown is an outdoor shot of that season's Jazz Band. The fall of 1988 brought some excitement within the ranks of the Thundering Herd when the group was invited to be the honor band at a political rally held at the Little Rock airport. President Ronald Reagan was there for a short touchdown visit campaigning for candidate George Bush. The photo below, which appeared in the Harding campus paper, the *Bison*, depicts the band performing at the event under the direction of drum major Terri Girdley Turner. As Reagan exited Air Force One onto the tarmac, the Bison Band played "Ruffles and Flourishes" followed by "Hail to the Chief." The second photo below is of Dr. Casey directing the Concert Band during a rehearsal; he earned his Ph.D. in music education from the University of Oklahoma that fall.

The 1989–90 Thundering Herd numbered about sixty in its ranks with field leadership by drum major Johnny Scott, and the Concert Band (*pictured at right above*) listed forty-five members. In the 1990 *Petit Jean* yearbook, percussionist Jennifer Brandon (*pictured above left*) said about being in the band: "It's a great way to make a lot of friends." Note: The football team won its last AIC crown that year with a 5–1 conference record and 7–4 overall. Unfortunately, they lost the first-round playoff game against Emporia State to end the season. The 1990–91 edition of the Thundering Herd below grew yet again to about sixty-five in the marching unit for home football games and area parades. Campus interest in the Jazz Band (*also shown below*) increased when the group backed up jazz great Vince Andrews during a special concert event at Harding.

The 1991–92 Thundering Herd played to the home crowd in the above photo during one of its halftime performances with an on-field presence of eighty students, whereas the Concert Band played its concerts with a strength of about fifty performers. The second photo presents that year's basketball Pep Band. On the front row in the photo below dressed in white trousers, drum major Colby Canterbury posed with the 1992–93 Thundering Herd for a yearbook shot. In another notation in the book about the Jazz Band, it stated that Dr. Warren Casey on occasion would perform on clarinet when he wasn't directing the group. The Thundering Herd is also shown below playing for a pep rally on campus.

In the fall of 1993, Harding alumnus Mark Hudson returned to the campus for a two-year stint as assistant band director. The above photos printed in the 1994 Harding yearbook show the Pep Band encircling their banner, which they proudly displayed at home basketball games in the Ganus Athletic Center (*at left*) and saxophone players Jon Sterling, Jenny Adamson, and Donna McMahan performing with the Concert Band during the groundbreaking ceremony for the McInteer Bible and World Missions Center on campus. In the photo below of the 1994–95 Thundering Herd, drum major Colby Canterbury stands on the front row extreme left. The head football coach was quoted in the yearbook as saying, "The band is really important to our momentum and enthusiasm. The timeliness of the noise provided by the band gives us an extra spark and motivation. That's a big part of the home field advantage. They get the crowd involved in the game. Without a band, ball games wouldn't be quite as much fun." The 1994–95 school year was the last year Harding played in the Arkansas Intercollegiate Conference.

The 1995–96 school year was Dr. Warren Casey's final term as director of the Thundering Herd and the Concert Band. His last marching unit was the one shown in the above left photo. Students of his are shown in the above right photo rehearsing on a Saturday morning at Alumni Field and putting on the finishing touches for a halftime show that afternoon. Note that Harding played intercollegiate athletics independently of any conference for the school years 1995–96 and 1996–97. The Harding basketball team (24–6) was the NAIA Southwest Region Champion in 1996 and qualified for the NAIA National Tournament.

For 1996–97 the new director of the Thundering Herd and the Concert, Jazz, and Pep Bands was Mike Chance, coming to the Harding campus with twenty-one years of experience directing bands in Texas public schools and his master's of music credentials. Dr. Warren Casey remained on the faculty teaching music courses and giving private lessons to students. The photos above depict the Pep Band at the Midnight Madness basketball game and the Symphonic Band (formerly the Concert Band) dressed up in their long dresses and tuxedos. The Harding basketball team finished the 1997 season 17–11 and qualified for the Southwest Region Tournament.

Mike Chance is shown above right in a photo from the 1998 Harding yearbook directing the Thundering Herd from the sideline in the band's traditional "HU" formation. The above left photo shows the 1997–98 Symphonic Band. In the fall of 1997, Dr. Warren Casey resumed the position of the Jazz Band director. The Pep Band that year played for basketball games held in the renovated Rhodes Memorial Field House rather than in the Ganus Athletic Center as in years past. The Harding athletic teams joined the Lone Star Conference in 1997 and played intercollegiate games in that conference for three years.

The greatest opportunity to happen in many years for the Music and Communications Departments at Harding came with the grand opening of the Donald W. Reynolds Center for Music and Communications in the fall of 1998. Filled with state-of-the-art networking and advanced design to contain sound, students and faculty alike were excited about the possibilities it would offer educationally. As expected, the band and choral divisions both performed at the event. The photo above left was taken during a halftime show of a 1998 Harding football game. Also pictured are members of the Symphonic Band presenting that year's Christmas Concert.

The above photos are from the 1999–2000 marching season of the Harding Thundering Herd. At left the senior drum major, Jay Larson, is finishing inspection of band members prior to their performing a halftime show that year. And at right, Gene Bates, Jennifer Sanders, and Hannah Sawyer do their part on the field putting on another entertaining presentation. In the top photo Cary Garner practices with that season's Symphonic Band. For the school year 2000–2001 Emily Smith (*seen below right*) served as the drum major of the Thundering Herd as band members (*left*) performed on the field at home football games. Beginning with the fall of 2000 Harding along with most of the other former members of the old Arkansas Intercollegiate Conference joined in to form the new Gulf South Conference for intercollegiate competition in all sports that each school fielded teams. As of this writing Harding is still a member of that conference. The third photo below features John Rogers and Brandon Tittle playing with the basketball Pep Band.

The above photo at left taken in the stands of Alumni Field on the Harding University campus shows the Thundering Herd Marching Band for 2001–02 led that season by drum majors Joe Bresnahan and Jared Holton. Clint Howard and Eric Colgrove stand at attention in the photo at right as the band prepares to entertain the crowd during a home football game. As in previous years, Mike Chance was the director of the Marching Band, the Symphonic Band, and the Orchestra, with Dr. Warren Casey conducting the Jazz Band. A student director was usually in charge of the Pep Band, with Chance as the advisor. The picture below left shows Harding's Thundering Herd trombone section in action during the halftime performance at Homecoming in 2002. Drum majors for the group that season were Joe Bresnahan and Brandon Tittle. At right are the Symphonic and Jazz Bands that performed on campus that year. The Bison football team ended with a 9–2 record that fall to post its best win-loss mark since the 1972 team finished 10–1.

Led in the stands and on the field by drum majors Brandon Tittle and Jonathan Schallert, the Thundering Herd (*in the above left photo*) plays the fight song at Homecoming 2003 for students and alumni. And the following January, members of the Pep Band join the Rhodes Rowdies in cheering on the Bison basketball team. For the uninitiated, "Rhodes Rowdies" refers to Harding fans who raise the roof at basketball games played on campus in Rhodes Memorial Field House. The top photo is of the 2003–04 Wind Ensemble.

Below (*lower left photo*), the 2004–05 Thundering Herd plays for the dedication of the new Center for Science and Engineering on the Harding campus. Also pictured are Director of Bands Mike Chance and that year's marching Thundering Herd in a group shot led by drum majors Jonathan Schallert and Katie Barker.

For the fall of 2005 the "Thunderin' Herd" took to the field in the newly carpeted First Security Stadium on campus; that is to say, the grass field was completely replaced with artificial turf, presenting a new challenge to football players and marching band members alike. Drum majors for the season were Katie Barker and Cassie Withrow. The school year also was the tenth season for director Michael Chance. It should be pointed out that in addition to his Marching and Concert Band duties that Chance was also responsible for the reemergence of the orchestra program on the school's campus during his tenure. Dr. Warren Casey also continued serving on the school's music staff as director of the Jazz Band.

Today Harding University, a member of the Division II Gulf South Athletic Conference, has over five thousand students on its campus, and it remains as one of only two private colleges or universities in Arkansas that maintains a music program that includes both a marching and concert band in its curriculum. Instrumental degrees include the Bachelor of Arts with a major in Music (Instrumental) and the Bachelor of Music Education (Instrumental). Harding alumni and friends look forward to a promising future for the school.

Afterword

As you can see, each one of the chapters of this book ends rather abruptly, and that is by design. For you see, this is not a novel. It is a book about real people, in real bands, at real universities. And their stories are ongoing; hence the chapters just stop, if only for a while, until the next pages are added to each band's history. In fact, they are being filled in to some degree on each campus as you read these very words.

I hope that you enjoy this book and that you will take some time out to go to a ballgame or to a special concert program where one of the college (or university) bands covered within these pages or on any other campus will be performing and enjoy the music they present. And take along someone else with you. You will be glad you went.

Acknowledgments

Many people are to be thanked for their unselfish time given over to me for this project. And I hope that I appropriately address them all here, though the human side of me says that I am inevitably going to leave someone out. But here goes . . .

On the Henderson State University campus, thanks go to David Rollins and Wendell Evanson, both former directors of that school's bands who read over my work of the Reddie Band and carefully critiqued the facts I have presented. Also, the librarians and archivists made available old yearbooks and a number of old photos from cataloged boxes that provided early glimpses of the school's past. Two histories of the school, *Henderson State University: Education since 1890,* by Bennie Gene Bledsoe, and *Henderson State College: The Methodist Years, 1890–1929,* by Dr. John Gladden Hall, were quite informative and I appreciate their perspectives of the campus. My sister, Lee, was a majorette in Evanson's band in the early 1970s, and I made sure that I had her nod of approval on that band's chapter. Finally, a patient of mine and a Reddie Band alumnus, Carl Long, kept me focused on the task at hand by routinely asking how this book was coming. With his and others' prodding, I did bring it to completion.

At the University of Central Arkansas, I appreciate the efforts of the current band director, Dr. Ricky Brooks, for procuring hard-to-find pictorial documentation for some of the seasons represented herein and for being so welcoming during my research visits and attendance at athletic events. The campus archives in Torreyson Library proved invaluable in referencing old yearbooks, school papers, and vintage photos, and I thank Jimmy Bryant and his staff for being so accommodating. I also enjoyed visiting with, albeit briefly, the former director Russell Langston and Homer Brown's daughter, Dr. Jackie Lamar. Special thanks to Louis Buehling for helping me to get some questions answered and to Mike Kemp and Polly Walter for making available select photos.

My visits to the University of Arkansas at Pine Bluff campus could not have been more informative and enlightening. I struck gold on meeting the distinguished and accomplished visual artist Dr. Henri Linton, and I mined every bit of information I could from him about that school and the band. His being in charge of the school's museum and the actual physical building of its displays afforded me access to peruse through literally mountains of memorabilia in his charge. Anyone who lives near or visits the UAPB campus simply must tour that school's museum. I also appreciate the visits and interviews I had with the current Director of Bands, John Graham, and his staff and their accommodating me with band photos and facts; they include James Horton, Gerome Hudson, Constance Castle, and Darrell Evans. Ziba Barber and Richard Redus also assisted me in locating select photos. No retelling of the UAPB Band story can be related without referencing *Must Be the Music,* a combination historical accounting and memoir of former band member Sederick C. Rice. Also important to me was Dr. U. G. Dalton's doctoral dissertation, entitled "The Music Department of the University of Arkansas at Pine Bluff. Its Development and Role in Music Education in the State of Arkansas, 1873–1973."

The Arkansas State University at Jonesboro is a most interesting campus these days in how it has grown over the years, especially since the days when I attended there for Dixie Band Camp in the mid-1960s. It is particularly comforting to see my friend, the late state senator Jerry Bookout, remembered with Bookout Circle for his decades-long work in fighting hard for the school. I would like to thank Dr. Brady Banta and his assistant, Malissa Davis, in ASU Archives and Special Collections for making old school publications available to me, including early campus yearbooks and journals. Within the Music

Department, I would like to acknowledge the assistance of the departmental chair and former band director, Dr. Tom O'Connor, and the band's recent director and current interim director, Ed Alexander and Kenneth Carroll, in their helping me to get facts straight. Plus my appreciation goes to a woman with a wealth of knowledge about ASU Band history and the willingness to share it, Ms. Sylvia Strawbridge. As luck would have it, I was able to connect with a friend from Band Camp days, who also was the daughter of a former A-State president and graduate of the campus itself and band alumna, Barbara Reng. Hearing her again was quite a blast from the past. Also, I would like to thank three other ASU Band alumni, Cindy Buehling (a public school music teacher and fellow church choir member), Dan Ross (Cindy's brother and ASU music faculty member), and John Irwin (former ASU drum major and current UCA choral director) for their regaling of stories about the ASU Band when Don Minx was its director—never a dull moment. Finally, two books about the campus proved most valuable in historical background for this book: they are *The ASU Story,* by Lee A. Dew, and *Voices from State,* by Larry Ball and William Clements.

The Arkansas Tech University story is personally a most interesting one partly because my mother and a few other relatives attended there. But even more so because of the consistently strong band program over the years. The Tech Band has the distinction of having had the fewest number of band directors on its podium since its inception. Only three people have ever been its Director of Bands—and each one has proved himself successful in that position. My thanks go out to the current director, Hal Cooper, for being so magnanimous in the times I spent with him and for his helpful comments in looking over the Tech chapter. His wife, Beth, was also most helpful since she keeps meticulous scrapbooks of Hal's work at the school. Thanks also go out to the staff at the Ross Pendergraft Library and Technology Center, especially for allowing me such open access to archival materials. *The History of Arkansas Tech University, 1909–1990,* by Kenneth Walker contains a motherload of information for the researcher and I appreciate having studied it. A trio of Tech Band supporters was most gracious in looking over my first draft of the band's chapter and I thank them for their time and comments. They are H. L. Shepherd (former director of Russellville High School Band), B. J. Dunn (insurance agent and avid band fan), and Dr. Robert Casey (former head of the school's Music Department). Those three kept me honest about Tech. Finally, I would like to acknowledge knowing three Tech alumnae and hearing their band stories at the school: Susan Antonetti (nee Byler), Susan Dunn (nee McIntyre), and Mary Ann Salmon (nee Sawyer).

Southern Arkansas University in Magnolia is a beautiful campus, which I enjoyed visiting, and its library proved most forthcoming with information for which I was looking. I would like to thank its staff, in particular Donna McCloy, who always knew the direction in which to go when I asked a question, and who physically walked me to a few places on campus where I might find the desired person I needed to visit. The school's current band director, J. P. Wilson, has led the group during a growth spurt for the program and obviously loves the work he is doing. I appreciate his time and efforts in getting the SAU chapter finished. Also helpful was the director of communications, Mark Trout, in the search for needed photos to flesh out current documentation of the band's story. Most informative was hearing SAU's retired history professor Dr. James Willis speaking at the Arkansas Historical Association's annual meeting on the origins of the four original Arkansas agricultural schools established in the state in 1909. He certainly filled in a lot of gaps for me, including bringing the Martin Bands to my attention. Incidentally, I look forward to seeing his history of SAU on which he is working. And lastly, I would like to thank fellow singer David Adcock for the few details he could remember about being in that band as a student in the 1970s.

I could not have come close to discovering as much information as I did about the University of Arkansas at Monticello Band if it had not been for the cooperation of the Special Collections staff headed up by Mary Heady at Taylor Library on the campus. She found stuff in places I never would have known to look, which I guess is her job, but she did it so pleasantly and willingly that I remain in her debt. The current band director at UAM, Gary Meggs, is an amazing motivator, recruiter, and musician, and I appreciate his time in getting the band's story accurate. I also very much enjoyed listening to his playing of his alto saxophone with a jazz combo here in Little Rock one night (man, can that guy play or what?!). Important in hearing about stories from the band's early years was a conversation I had with the daughter of Lee Wallick, Peggy Jeter, and I enjoyed it immensely.

Marvin Lawson was a most pleasant gentleman to communicate with while I was researching the Ouachita Baptist University Band chapter. He read my first draft very closely and cordially made comments when appropriate. And he even scanned photos he thought I might need and mailed them to me at times. If all sources were as resourceful as he was, then research would not be as time-consuming as it can be. Regarding the school's history, Michael Arrington's *Ouachita Baptist University: The First 100 Years* proved to be a most informative read. I also appreciate the visits I had with Dr. Craig Hamilton and Robert Hesse, the current chair of Instrumental Music, and athletic band director, respectively. A real treat was visiting and conversing with the state's composer laureate, Dr. W. Francis McBeth, still a frequent visitor to the campus, even though he is officially retired from the institution (he told me that he still works at his church and at composing most every day); and I owe him big-time for agreeing to write the Fanfare for this book. I would also like to acknowledge the cooperation of the staff at the Rile-Hickingbotham Library for their assistance in accessing research materials. It was so interesting to visit a campus where close to one in ten students are involved in the band program. Finally, I would like to thank my friend, Arthur "Chip" Broadbent, for his recollections about the OBU Band, even though he was in the choir program during his years on campus.

Folks at Harding University were most hospitable to me during the times I spent on their campus in research and in watching and listening to the band in performances. Here's to Michael Chance, the school's current band director, and to the excellence he and others on the school's faculty expect and obtain from the students enrolled in the music program. The library personnel at Brackett Library were most cordial to my research requests and I appreciate their patience with the hours I kept in the building. I also would like to thank the various band members who gave me their undivided attention while I asked unending questions. But, perhaps the single most informative source regarding the Harding Band's history was "Harding University Department of Music: A History," written by Jason Jewell in the completion of his Master's Thesis from Pepperdine University and later edited by Arthur Shearin and printed in a booklet format. That information was invaluable to me.

In addition, I would like thank Dr. Brooks Blevins for his assistance with information about the history of the instrumental program at Lyon College when it was known as Arkansas College and for being able to reference his book about the school, *Lyon College, 1872–2002: The Perseverance and Promise of an Arkansas College.*

Other books that helped with the perspective of instrumental music in Arkansas colleges over the years were *Hendrix College: A Centennial History,* and the early history of the University of Arkansas at Little Rock, *The People's College,* both by James E. Lester Jr.; the John Brown University history, *Head, Heart and Hand,* by Rick Ostrander; *Arkansas Baptist College: A Historical Perspective, 1884–1982,* by Vertie L. Carter; and *Two Centuries of Methodism in Arkansas, 1800–2000,* by Nancy Britton.

Appreciation is further extended to the library staffs at Hendrix College, the University of Arkansas at Little Rock, Philander Smith College, and the Butler Center of the Central Arkansas Library System in Little Rock; all of them made available important photos used herein. And I very much enjoyed the short time I spent with Charles "Chuck" Booker as he proudly spoke of the growth of the Music Department at the University of Arkansas at Fort Smith.

This project could not have been brought to conclusion without the editing prowess of Debbie Self and the publication smarts of John Coghlan at Phoenix International, Inc. Special thanks to both of them. And I would like to offer my utmost appreciation to Joe D. Nichols for helping me to see the "big picture" and to Brandon Creek for his "scholarly" graphic talents.

The last thank you's I would like to express are to my parents, Everett and Lee Thompson, who have been most encouraging to me in this project and who dog-sat with the incredible Mr. Trix during my many trips across this state; to my office assistant, Christopher Arnold, who kept the trains running appropriately so that I could pursue this book; to Tom and Linda Hitt, who have shown me incredible hospitality and friendship during the pursuit of my writing these two books about bands in Arkansas; and to other family members and friends who have been so patient with me when I opted not to spend time with them during these projects. I promise to do better.

About the Author

T. T. Tyler Thompson, a member of the University of Arkansas Razorback Band from 1967 to 1971, graduated from the University of Arkansas in Fayetteville with a Bachelor of Arts in Chemistry and German. After teaching in public schools in Pine Bluff and North Little Rock, he enrolled at the University of Houston College of Optometry, where he received his Bachelor of Science and Doctor of Optometry degrees. Since 1982 Thompson has resided in Little Rock, where he practices optometry and edits optometric publications. He is also the author of *The University of Arkansas Razorback Band: A History, 1874–2004.*

Index

Hesse, Robert, xviii, 333, 334
Hicklin, LeeAnna, 242
Hill, Gary, 197
Hill, Mr. and Mrs. Gus, 336
Hill, Monty, 32
Hinkle, Lewis, 277
Hinson, Lee, 69, 70
Hogue, Lisa, 237
Holder, Steven, 352
Holland, Billie Jean, 55
Holley, Bankie, 290
Hollis, Rashad, 116
Holmes, Tiffany, 286
Holton, Jared, 366
"Homer's Heroes," xix, 69, 73
Hood, Edna, 165, 166
Hooper, Mary Ann, 226
Hope, Bob, 321
Hope, Perry, 182
Hoppe, William A., 302, 303
Hopper, Chris, 149
Horn, Jerry, xxiii
Horn, John, 128
Howard, Clint, 366
Howard, James Paul, 172
Hudson, Jerome, 110
Hudson, Mark, 354, 355, 362
Humphrey, Vice Pres. H. H., 64
Hurley, Sylvia, 166
Husak, Thomas, 277
Hutchinson, Jo, 258

I

Inzer, Ronnie, 18
Irman, Cindy, 196

J

Jackson, Ray, 62
Jarnigan, Lawrence, 218
Jazz Rock Stage Band, 24
Jewell, Jason, 336, 339, 340, 343, 347
Johns, Cheri, 198
Johnson, Arthur, 112
Johnson, Christopher, 113, 114
Johnson, Joel, 77
Johnson Sr., Johnny B., 102
Johnson, Pres. Lyndon B., 64
Jones, Clarence, 96
Jones, George C., 3
Jones, Mrs. W. M., 208
Jordon, Al Gene, 173

Joyner, George, 93
Joyner, John, 83
Justiss, J. E. (Jimmie), 214, 217–20

K

Kalnins, Richard, 357
Kappa Kappa Psi, 33, 38, 74, 79, 101, 114, 140, 182, 230, 273, 275, 281, 283–85, 288, 325, 332
Kays, V. C., 122
Keener, Eric, 249
Keeter, Shawn, 38
Kelley, Orville, 16, 17
Kendricks, Joe, 265
Kennedy, Pres. John F., 63, 137
Key, Tiffany, 332
Kiilsgaard, Robert, 81
King Jr., James Nelson, 274
Kirk, Leonard, 340
Konikoff, Ben, 216
Koskowski, David, 276, 278
Kramer, Donald, xv, 25

L

Laas, William, 341, 342
Ladd, Jon, 196
Laing, Millard, 12
Langford, David, 240, 242
Langston, Russell, xix, 71–78
Lanier, Veronica, 205, 206
Larson, Jay, 365
Lavin, Thomas, 302
Law, Chuck, xv
Lawson, Marvin, xviii, 313–24
Ledbetter, Leigh, 153, 154
Lee, Claude Rogers, 350
Leet, Robert, 130
Leflar, Robert, xi, xii
Leslie, Willis "Convoy," 287
Levya, Jesse, 41
Lewis, Stanford, 280
Lewis, Tracy, 237
Linder, John, 188
Linder, Mary Alice, 55, 306
Linton, Marion, 172
Linvall, Hales, 173
Lisemby, Greg, 244–46
Little Symphony, 65
Loring, Kevin, 114
Lovell, Austin, 181
Lowe, Danny L., 238
Luck, James T., 310, 313

Lyle, George, 131
Lynch, Brandon, 117

M

Macchiarolo, Beth, 31
Madlock, Kim, 327
Mahling, Otto, xxi, 252, 253
Majors, Billy, 276
Maness, Larry, 136, 137
Marcato Club, 230
Mars, Jearl, 185
Martel, G. G. (Glen), 212–14
Martin Bands, xvii
Martin, Cari, 330
Martin, Elizabeth, 173
Martin, Fred D., xvii, 301
Martin, Gary, 239
Martin, Richard, 228
Martin, William C., 307
Mays, Rod, 325
Mazoch, Jenna, 332
McAllister, Bruce, 110
McAnally, Kent, 28
McBeth, W. Francis, ix, xviii, 26, 196, 310–13, 316, 318, 320, 329
McBryde, Ashley, 159, 160
McCarty, Jimmy, 147
McCauley and His Serenaders, 298
McCauley, Wayne, 299
McClung, Zach, 39
McCollum, JoAnn, 276
McCuin, Kelley, 117
McFarlin, Adam, 40
McGee, Shelton, 98
McGinty, Matt, 204
McIntyre, Susan, 194
McMahan, Donna, 362
McMorella, Elizabeth, 218
McMurry, Mac, 329
McVinney, Barry, 328
Meggs, Gary, xxi, 282, 289, 290
Mells, David, 89
Melton, Ellis, 313, 314
Mendenhall, Logan, 209
Merrill Jr., Alger Lee, 301
Mickey, Sarah, xxi, 247
Mikita, Andrew, 52
Miller, Brent, 289
Miller, Joseph, 109, 110
Miller, Mrs. Leora Pryce, 294
Mills, J. B., 224

Minton, Ira, 209
Minx, Donald R., xx, 134–48
Mitchell, Harold, 16
Moix, Chris, 37
Moods, The, 345
Moody, Fannie Marie, xxi, 337
Moore, Doug, 142, 143
Moore, Erle T., 343, 347
Morrill Act, xviii, 86
Morris, Leonard, 171
Moss, Stephen, 38
Moyers, Charles, 129
Mullenax, Tim, 287
Must Be the Music, 89

N

Nance, Nena, 197
Nash, Johnny, 352, 353
Neal, Christopher, 110, 111
Needham, Bobby Jim, 178
Neely, Mrs. Joseph, 87
Nelson, Nina, 111
Nichols, Becky, 275
Nix, Robin, 62
Nixon, Pres. Richard, 68

O

O'Connor, Thomas, 148–51
Odom, Orin, 117
Oliver, George, 345
Oliver, Private, 11
Oliver, Richard O., xx, 222–33, 239
O'Neal, Tom, 153–55, 157
Orr, Professor, 338
Ouachibones, 328
Overstreet, Charles, 218
Owen, Don, 184
Owen, Syble, 60

P

Pace, Ginny, 21
Pack, Les, 290
Parker, Don, 110
Parker, Philip, 195
Patterson, Hugh, 7
Patty, James L., 130, 131
Peevey, Neal, 138
Peterson, Steven, 76
Phelps, Bill, 66
Philo Ragtime Band, 296
Pitner, Martha, 348

Sutterfield, Rita, 323
Swain, Sherry, 190
Symphonette, 344

T
Talbot, Anna, 150
Tapp, L. B., xvii
Tau Beta Sigma, 33, 38, 74, 79, 81, 101, 110, 140,
    182, 230, 274, 281, 283, 325
Taylor, Dallas, 82
Taylor, J. William, 294
Taylor, Novis, 217
Thomas, Searcy, 268
Thompson, Betty, 178
Thompson, Frances, 266
Thompson, L. C., 48
Tiger Blast/Tunes/Jam, 333, 334
Tittle, Brandon, 365–67
Todenhoft, Norman, 136
Tophatters, 51, 53, 56, 58, 63
Torres, Al, 249
Towers, Jim, 282
Tribe, The, 138, 141, 157
Trusler, Milton, 53–57
T-Steppers, 60
Tucker, Stacy, 197
Tull, James A., 7
Turk, Euna, 186
Turnbow, Sherry, 148
Turner, Charles R., 51
Turner, Terry Girdley, 357, 359
Two Centuries of Methodism in Arkansas, 2
Tyler, Tyrone, 101

U
Umholtz, Paige, 326

V
Vallo, Victor, 243
Vardeman, Ray, 279, 280, 317
Varsitonians, The, 220, 222, 225, 227, 228
Vaughn, Dennis, 272, 273
Vaughn, Steve, 154, 155
Voices from State, 122
Voyles, Felicia, 359

W
Wainwright, Joan, 190
Walker, Charles A., 108
Walker, Richard, 79
Walker, Thomas B., 11

Wall, Mutt, 257
Wallace, Mark, 77
Wallick, C. A., 253
Wallick, Lee Opha, xvii, xxi, 253–63
War Party, 153, 156
Ward, Elizabeth, 194
Warner, Ben, 112, 114
Warner-Krewson, 122
Washington, Kelvin, 110, 111
Watkins, Elaine, 190
Watson, Jack, 7
Watson, John Brown, 88, 90, 92
Watson, R. B. "Scrubby," xvii
Watts, Christi, 328
Weller, Kirk, 281
Wesly, David, 202
West, Adam, 221
Widner, John, 195
Wilber, John, 105
Wilhelmi, Jeremy, 205
Wilkins, Jay, 29
Williams, Dona, 227
Williams, Gloria, 272
Williams, John E., 90, 93
Williams, Nathaniel, 117
Williamson, Marvin, xx, 162–78
Willis, Joe, 257
Willis, Susan, 354
Willson, Meredith, xvii
Wilson, J. P., xx, 247–49
Wilson, Thomas, 286
Wilson, Wayne K., 268
Wisner, Ralph, 125
Witherspoon, Gene, xx, 178–92
Witherspoon, Jill, 186
Withrow, Cassie, 368
Wolfe, Jerry, 354
Womack, J. P., 208
Wood, Jack, 183
Wood, Joe, 14
Workman, Eliza Harris, 6
Workman, James W., 6
Workman, Steve, 190
Worley, Brent, 82
Worman, Harold, 138
Wortham, Jeremy, 160
Wray, Ron, 244
Wyrick, Hal, 176

Y
Youngblood, Curtiss, 214

"Best Wishes + all the love + honor to UAPB / AM;N"
..... Rodney D. Chm

Nince Meet you

U.A.P.B. 06